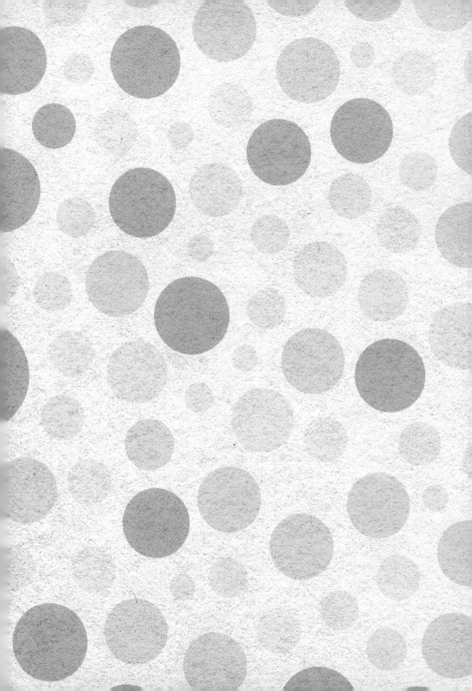

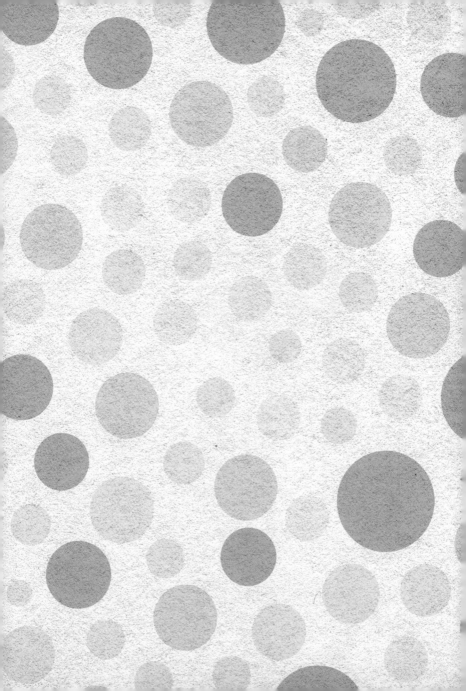

GirlCode

GirlCode

A SINGLE GIRL'S

~~~ Guide to ~~~

SEX & DATING

~~~ by ~~~

Laura Murphy
Sachi Ezura
Brooke VanPoppelen
Wenonah Hoye
Chelsea White

Table of

Contents

Intro

Jessimae Peluso

Girl Code is the pink and glittery glue that keeps women together.

When we were little, we all knew exactly what our parents meant when they told us to "be a good girl." Whether aggressively whispered at a restaurant or barked at us before being dragged to visit that great aunt we really didn't want to see, the rules were pretty clear: be respectful to grown ups, always say please and thank you, brush your hair, and for the love of God keep your skirt down.

Then we got to junior high, where boys and hormones collide in a potent cocktail we call puberty, and suddenly being a "good girl" got a whole lot more complicated. Enter Girl Code. Never openly discussed until now, Girl Code is like a secret language that exists between girls. It's in our DNA. It's how we know the difference between a bestie and a frenemy (a bestie will tell us those jeans make us look fat when they do, a frenemy will imply they make us look fat when they don't). Or what to do when our best friend's crush tells his friend to tell us that he thinks we're cute (tell him we're not interested, obvs . . . unless he's super cool and we liked him first anyway).

Girl Code has likely existed since the first Paleolithic slumber party happened in a cave 2.5 million years ago. We can imagine the grunted gossip about Lucy stepping to Olga's boyfriend, followed by tears and insults, which eventually gave way to all the cave girls brushing each other's hair with rocks and telling one another they looked pretty—even though everyone secretly thought Lucy looked fat in her mammoth-skin nightgown. Thus, Girl Code was born and over the next several eons, it was sculpted and refined as mothers, daughters, sisters, and girlfriends passed the Code down across millions of generations of women.

GIRL CODE THROUGH THE AGES

THE FIRST WALK OF SHAME	ORIGIN OF THE SLUT	UNFORTUNATE DISCOVERY OF STDs
200 MILLION B.C.	6000 B.C.	800 B.C.

Being a single girl in this world is more complicated than ever. We have to be smart and strong and independent—and look good at the same time. On top of that, social media has catapulted us into an age where sex and dating happen both online and off, and we have to know how to handle ourselves in both those worlds. It's easy to overthink every word we utter and every gesture and decision we make. (*Should we have sent that text? Should we order that cheeseburger? Is this shirt too slutty... or not slutty enough?*) Although, Girl Code can't answer all of life's tricky questions for you, it *will* guide you when you are gripped by uncertainty, instill in you the confidence to make those hard choices, and be the supportive big sister who'll make you laugh through your tears when you've really screwed up.

Carly Aquilino

Girl Code is just unwritten rules that girls have to follow so that they will still have friends ... and boyfriends.

BEGINNING OF AWKWARD CONDOM CONVERSATIONS	MASTURBATION DECLARED AWESOME	FRIENDS ADD BENEFITS	FIRST MAN LANDS IN THE FRIEND ZONE
THE MIDDLE AGES	18TH CENTURY	1926	1969

In other words, we won't tell you how to be a "good girl," but we will help you be good at being a girl. Girl Code is less a strict set of rules than a roadmap to being the best girl you can be. Whatever rules there may be are flexible—and they don't apply at all when you have your period. Living the Code is being awesome without making other girls hate you. It's never settling for less than what you deserve. It's knowing how your body works, so you can teach him how to work it (for the greater good of all girls). It's once in a while letting guys think they're the smart ones (but not too often). It's finding the humor in your mistakes. And most importantly, it's going to bed at night feeling good about who you are. (Sometimes the 'keep your skirt down' rule still applies—but only sometimes.)

Tanisha Long

Girl Code is what I do every day so I can respect myself as a person.

SPYING ON A CRUSH GOES TOO FAR	BREAK-THROUGHS IN FOREPLAY	GREAT, NOW ONLINE DATING?	GIRL CODE
1975	1994	2003	PRESENT DAY

Shalyah Evans

It's how to be a lady without pissing off other ladies. Girl Code will keep the ladies on your side so you're not a lone she-wolf.

Occasionally, we make poor choices and hopefully we learn from them. But, through it all, we share our experiences with other girls and stick together—it's a jungle out there, so we have to have each other's backs. Through the wisdom of Girl Code, you can learn to get through any situation with as little drama, embarrassment, and awkwardness as possible. Because it's not about what you did the night before, it's about owning it the next day. Girl Code.

Masturbation

Sachi Ezura

I had a friend who discovered
her orgasm by grinding up against
her stuffed animals.

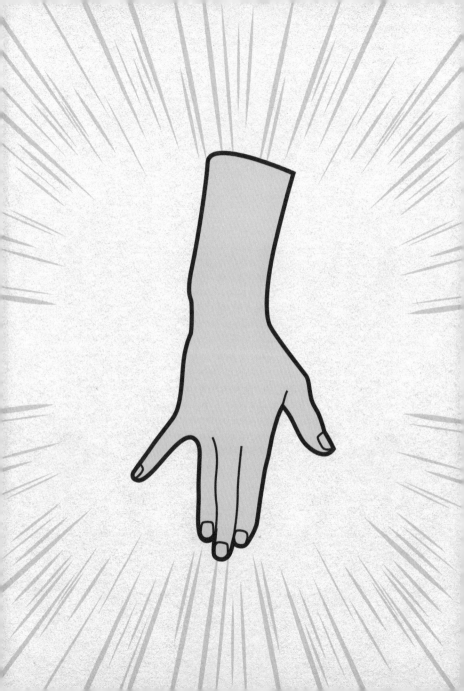

Alice Wetterlund

Masturbation is super important for girls. It's up there with voting.

 f I were President of the United States of America, my first act in office would be to get every girl a therapist and a vibrator. It would alleviate a lot of the world's problems. Happy women = happy world.

I strongly believe that you can't know what you like sexually until you (ahem) get in touch with yourself. When I was in high school, there was this really popular girl—let's call her Tiffany. Tiffany was known for doing lots of sexy stuff, but she claimed that she never masturbated. "Why would I do that when I could get a guy to do it for me?" Um, maybe because it feels better than a sixteen-year-old boy fumbling around down there like there's dust in his Nintendo 64. Maybe because there's no risk of STDs or getting pregnant or having to listen to him whine about how now you owe him something in return. Maybe because why the fuck not?

Sure, it's fun to go out there and try to meet someone or to have a night out with your girlfriends, but more often than not, the perfect night can be had with a bottle of Pinot Grig, a box set of _Downton Abbey_ and two AA batteries.

ONE

The Early Days: If you're a young woman who's never done it, do not feel embarrassed. In the words of your gross health teacher, masturbation is perfectly natural. Take a night when your parents are out of the house and try a bunch of stuff. Most importantly, you'll need to find your clitoris. It shouldn't be difficult because it's front and center and it feels magical when you touch it. Now, *how* you touch it is up to you.

When I first started, I did not immediately see what the big deal was. I would feel around down there and nothing felt particularly arousing. Then, one night in the bath, I discovered that if I contorted my body so my crotch was directly under the faucet I could achieve sexual bliss. (Author's note: had I forgotten to lock the door, it also could have been the perfect angle for extreme embarrassment.) I had a friend who discovered her orgasm by grinding up against her stuffed animals. Another found it accidentally by sitting on her parents' laundry machine. You'll never know what gets your jollies off until you try, so experiment.

Jamie Lee

I have a friend who's like, "I just never masturbate." I'm like, "You do realize it feels like pizza tastes?"

Girl Meets Toy: I can't tell you *how* to masturbate, because it's different for every girl. But if you haven't tried it with a vibrator, you might be missing out on the best experience of your life. I bought my first vibrator when I was a junior in high school. My girlfriends and I went to Miami for our first real spring break. Since a lot of firsts were happening that spring (first fake ID, first fake ID confiscated, etc.), we decided it was time for all of us to have a good old-fashioned sexual awakening. So my girlfriends and I headed to Ricky's and purchased matching vibrators. None of us knew what we were doing, but I was pissed when my friend Jenn took the pink one and I was stuck with lame-ass purple. Turns out when it's down there, you don't even notice what color it is. All you notice is that it feels freakin' awesome.

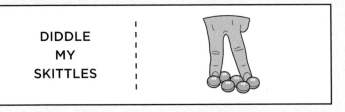

DIDDLE
MY
SKITTLES

Now, with the help of the Internet, you can purchase sex toys without awkwardly asking the cashier for a receipt with your Magic Pulsating Wand. Find a lady-friendly store with customer reviews and get shopping! (Babeland.com is a site designed for females that even has sections like Beginners and Waterproof.) Tip from your friendly writer: if you live with your parents or roommates, look for something quiet. Back when I was an amateur at this stuff, I bought the cheapest vibrator I could find, but when I brought it home, it sounded like I was operating a chain saw. Suffice it to say, my mom was under the impression I did a lot of woodworking that summer.

April Rose

I don't like the word 'masturbation.'
I like to call it 'petting the kitty.'

Nicole Byer

You gotta know how your body works. If you don't know how it works, he's not going to know how it works, and then you're just not going to get anything worked.

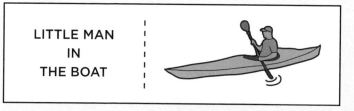

LITTLE MAN
IN
THE BOAT

If you live with people, you're going to have to institute some measures to maintain your privacy. Put on some loud music, not so loud that you won't be able to hear someone sneaking up behind you. If you need visual stimulation (aka porn) to get going, set your Safari to "Private Browsing" or Chrome to "Incognito." (That's how ubiquitous masturbation is in our society—your Internet browser basically WANTS you to masturbate.) Always keep a second browser window behind your porn-filled browser window in case someone comes up behind you and be ready with that CTRL + W. If you need to download some stuff and keep it on your computer, label it with something no one will ever look at like "Grandma's Spa Trip Photos."

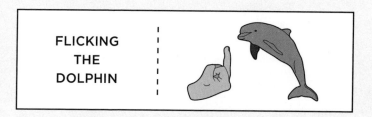

FLICKING
THE
DOLPHIN

A word on porn: it doesn't do it for everyone. And most of it is made for guys. When I was a teenager, everything on the Internet was way too intense for me and did not give me any happy downstairs feelings. The spectrum of what turns girls on is far wider than the average guy—you might need something visual or something more verbal, something wilder or something tamer. Try reading *Fifty Shades of Grey*, thinking about the hot busboy at your favorite restaurant, or watching that scene in *The Departed* where Leo rips Vera Farmiga's panties off and does the dirty to Pink Floyd's "Comfortably Numb." (Don't act like you don't know exactly what scene I'm talking about.) The Internet is full of super hard-core stuff and if it's not your bag, find something that is.

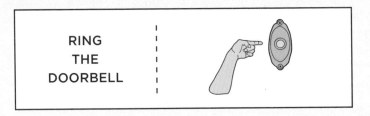

RING
THE
DOORBELL

Your Boyfriend's Worst Enemy: A lot of guys see masturbating as similar to pooping—normal for guys, inconceivable for girls. I remember being asked whether I'd ever masturbated during a co-ed game of Truth or Dare and feeling mortified. What would these guys think of me if they knew I was engaging in this heinous act? If they had asked a guy, the answer would have been "Duh, yes." But for some reason, for me, it was a terrifying moment where I was certain if I told the truth, I'd be exiled from the party and forced to wear the scarlet letter M. I took the Dare and licked a stick of deodorant instead. Phew—crisis averted!

Guys are very easily threatened. They like to believe they have value. They don't want to think they can be replaced by a silicon tube or a large zucchini. And the truth is, they can't. A vibrator can't hold you at night. A vibrator can't take you to prom or comfort you during scary movies. Your dad doesn't want to give away his only daughter to marry a vibrator. However, because a vibrator can do one thing that guys can't—namely, vibrate—guys get all squeamish and sad if they think you've found a substitute for their favorite extremity.

Carly Aquilino

I talk about masturbating all the time with my friends. We call it DJing. It's like a little code word. Sometimes I call my friend Ashley and I'll be like, "Hey what'd you do last night?" And she's like, "I was DJing all night. I was spinning it on the ones and twos."

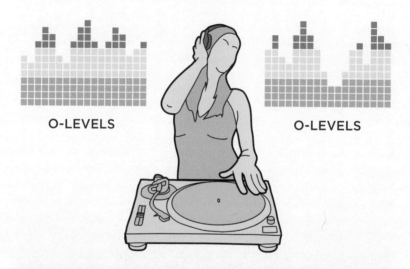

O-LEVELS   O-LEVELS

NEW TERMS FOR MASTURBATION

Playing Yahtzee
Blogging
Pushing the red button
Thinking 'bout Channing
Fingering a perp
Tiddlywinks
Handling some business

Being your own best friend
Phoning home
Holding court
Becoming more self-aware
Touch football
Reading a
Nicholas Sparks novel

We all know our boyfriends are jerking off when we're not around. Girls have come to terms with this. It's time we let our boyfriends in on the secret that we too need some alone time. If he finds your me-time toys or asks you point blank if you ever masturbate, let him in on the secret strategically. Explain that while you'll always prefer sexy time with him, occasionally he's not around to do what you want done. You can even send him a sexy text while you're doing it, "Thinking of you…" How can he be threatened when he knows he's the one on your mind?

The bottom line is if you don't know your body well, it's time to get to know your body. There are far too many girls out there who are sexy as hell but not comfortable being sexual. We live in an advanced society where women can do everything men can do— run for president, walk on the moon, lead a Fortune 500 company. It's time to level the playing field in jacking off too. Ladies, stand with me! Raise one hand in the air in solidarity and stick the other one down your pants. Don't deny yourself your happy time. Become a master masturbator today.

GirlCode:

REACH OUT AND TOUCH YOURSELF.

Rebounding

Laura Murphy

Everyone warns you about catching feelings
for a rebound, but nobody talks about the
dangers of fabricating feelings.

Tanisha Long

You gotta get under somebody to get over somebody, right?

Rebounding is the shit. We all know that. When properly executed it is the post-breakup miracle bra your deflated ego needs. The Girl Code to rebounding is clear-cut: get in, get it in, and when you feel you've won the fight against loneliness, get out.

Unfortunately, it's not always that simple. Complications can arise in the form of clingy guys or worse, feelings. For instance, what do you do if you accidentally end up in another relationship and the dude you are using to fill the hole (figuratively and literally) that your ex left behind ends up dumping you, too? Can you rebound from the rebound? Can you threebound?

I used to think I was really good at rebounding. Amidst the drama and pain of an emotional breakup there would be moments when I would contemplate all the people I could potentially rebound with; flirty coworkers, hot guys on the subway, the hot guy that worked at Subway. I would actually start to get excited about the breakup. Now I realize why. I was never the one being dumped. Which means I wasn't really rebounding in the true sense. I was just using breakups as an excuse to be whorey. Which was fun, too. But then I got dumped for real and learned an invaluable lesson on the right and wrong way to make yourself feel better.

HOUSE CALL

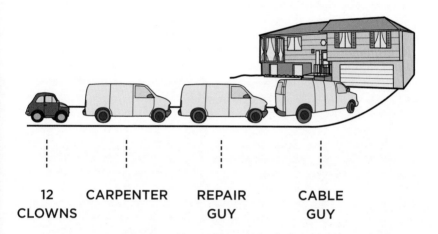

| 12 CLOWNS | CARPENTER | REPAIR GUY | CABLE GUY |

Jessimae Peluso

You break up with a dude, who cares? Cable guy's coming over. Bang him on the door of the dishwasher. Break that shit off, have to call another guy. Sleep with him on the table, have to call a carpenter. Rebound with that guy. Improvise.

It started out as a classic story:

Girl meets boy with shaved head and Irish accent.

Girl and boy fall in love.

Boy leaves the country suddenly and sends an email breaking up with girl.

A week later girl fills bald-shaped void in her heart and hoo-ha with less attractive, but equally hairless English boy with crooked teeth.

Yeah. I lowered my standards a little. Whatever. We've all been there. Teeth can be fixed. But instead of just riding it/him out and moving on to being single like I should have, I broke Girl Code big time and convinced myself I really liked him. It was partially because I missed my ex and partially because I didn't want to feel like I was wasting time. I hate wasting time.

SIGNS THAT YOU'RE JUST SOMEBODY'S REBOUND

Your birthday present was a wig and a mask

His idea of kinky: pretend to be the love of his life

He's pretty big into crying

He seems to be in two places at once—and both are her Instagram

You caught him staring at the hollow nothingness on the horizon

He introduces you as his "pointless temporary sex partner"

Nicole Byer

You should not talk to your rebound about your ex. You can't ride someone and be like, "He was so good to me until he wasn't." That's not cute.

DON'T TALK ABOUT YOUR EX
WHEN YOU'RE HAVING SEX

Everyone warns you about catching feelings for a rebound. But nobody talks about the dangers of fabricating feelings. As girls, sometimes we are too smart for our own good and being able to think ourselves into things is a real danger. Our minds are so powerful that there are actual cases of girls thinking themselves into being "pregnant." They look pregnant and feel pregnant, but then they give birth to an air baby and everyone realizes they were just delusional. That's some powerful mind shit. It is also straight crazy. We should be harnessing this power and using it for good, not wasting it on fake pregnancies and crap relationships. Nonetheless, there I was making myself believe that this off-brand version of my ex-boyfriend could be the one. Deluded and broken, I focused all my energy on him. He promptly broke up with me for being too needy.

Shalyah Evans

You're not looking for your future husband. You are looking for someone to bang the sadness out of you.

The only thing that stings more than being dumped is being dumped by a guy for whom you settled in the first place. With my ego fully in the gutter I did the only thing I could think of and sought solace in the next shiny noggin I bumped into. After threebounding with an accentless dude who looked like Popeye, I realized the bald thing had now become a full-blown fetish. I was screwed. And for some reason each successive guy was getting shorter, like when you clone something too many times and the genes get watered down. How had I gotten here? Would I ever be attracted to a guy with great hair again? Who was I? What did I even want? I couldn't remember. That's when it occurred to me that no amount of attention from even the hottest hairless guy in the world was going to make me feel better about myself.* I needed to do that on my own, alone, for more than just a week or a month.

*This is not all the way true. Attention from Jason Statham, Kelly Slater, or Channing Tatum probably would've made me feel better.

I AM WOMAN

Jessimae Peluso

I talked about my ex to my rebound and he was like, "You need to get over that." So I was like, "I will heal at my own pace. I am woman hear me roar." And he was like, "I am man, I will leave."

So to answer the question I posed in the beginning, can you rebound from a rebound? Sure. You can also rob banks to get over a shoplifting problem. But all it will get you is a longer prison sentence. In other words, the more times you rebound, the harder it is to get back in touch with who you are. Confidence comes from independence and being by yourself is way underrated . . . unless you're by yourself in prison. I imagine that would suck.

The get in/get out Girl Code to rebounding still stands, but it's just the first phase in the healing process. How you handle it and its aftermath will determine how long it will take you to get over the breakup that spawned this sexual band-aid in the first place. If you want to avoid dragging this shit out forever: in between sexed-up romps with the reboundee, get back in touch with your friends, your hobbies, and the things you liked about yourself when you were single. And don't be afraid to be alone, even if you spend some of that time crying. If you threebound you might end up with a fetish and never, ever think yourself into being fake pregnant (that's really just common sense).

GirlCode:

THE WRONG GUY IS THE RIGHT GUY.

Online Dating

Brooke Van Poppelen

It's getting late, there are no sparks flying, and I feel like an idiot for buying a new outfit and shaving my pubes.

April Rose

Online dating is completely normal. It used to be creepy and you didn't know who was really on it, but now everyone does it.

 notification pops up on my iPhone. I have a message from the cute guy I have been getting to know via an online dating service. The thrill of a potential date washes over me and in that moment nothing else matters. I stop in the middle of the street, standing there like an idiot while pedestrians bump into me and give me the evil eye.

Yup. I confess. I'm an online dater. For a while it seemed like the last thing I would ever do but I ran out of cute baristas to hit on, so here we are. Truth is, everyone is online dating and let's be honest—it's the most effective way to know who's single and ready to mingle! There's a rush to putting together a profile and then seeing who checks it out. You exchange a few messages and next thing you know—the date is on! Where it goes from there is another story completely, but I'm in it to win it.

I feverishly log into my account as "WhiskeyHurricane" (classy, I know).

Jeff_Austin2Brooklyn says: "I'm going to be in your neighborhood tonight for this thing I have with some friends until 9 pm, but when I'm done we could grab a beer if you're down."

SHOPPING FOR A BRO

SHOPPING FOR A BRA

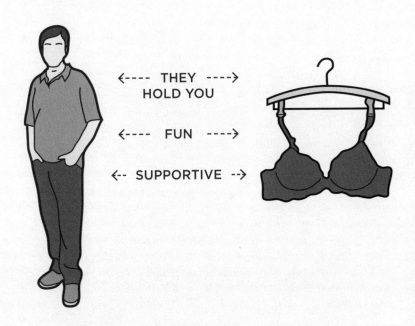

←---- THEY ----→
HOLD YOU

←---- FUN ----→

←-- SUPPORTIVE -→

Tanisha Long

Girls like to use online dating because we want to find a guy the same we find our favorite bra. We just want our boobs to be held by somebody fun and supportive.

I AM SO DOWN, YOU DON'T EVEN KNOW!!!, is what I am screaming in my head. But I play it cool and write back a calm and detached message that doesn't let on that I have already convinced myself Jeff_Austin2Brooklyn is, in fact, my future husband.

WhiskeyHurricane says: "I think that could work. (OH, IT IS GOING TO WORK.) I also have something with friends 'til about 9 pm (THIS IS A LIE, I WILL BE OBSESSING OVER MY OUTFIT AND MAKEUP) then I could do something with you. (I WANT TO DO EVERYTHING WITH YOU, ALWAYS.) Hit me up closer to the time and we'll see what's up. (I WILL BE STARING AT MY PHONE WAITING FOR YOUR TEXT FOR AT LEAST TWO HOURS.)

The rush of knowing that IT IS ON for tonight rewires my brain and changes my plans for the entire day. I get ready to say goodbye to single life because this time, this time, this fucking Internet dating thing is going to work out. It HAS to work out.

I have work to do today, but instead I veer into Forever 21 since it is now more important than ever to finally reinvent myself. I begin hunting for an outfit that is cute but not trying too hard. I need to seem like I always look effortlessly adorable in a romper. Okay. On second thought, no romper. Back away from the romper. A sundress and denim jacket? I don't know. That's so Kelly Clarkson. I want more edge than that but don't want to look like Miley Cyrus at the VMAs. Kristen Stewart has impeccable style. What would K-Stew wear?

This goes on for well over an hour. I end up buying the exact sort of outfit that I would buy anyhow and leave Forever 21 minus a new image but hey, now I've got a new skirt and top.

How many hours do I have 'til we meet? Five? Okay. I can pull off a pedicure I just have to remember to leave myself enough time for hair and makeup.

I'm at Dashing Diva spending more money that I don't have on a pedicure, but it will pay off when Jeff_Austin2Brooklyn sees how put together I am. I swear the women painting my toenails are making fun of me in a different language

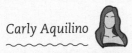

Carly Aquilino

It's okay to tell little lies on your profile, but make sure that it's nothing too crazy. Don't brag about how nice and big your house is if you forget to mention that it's filled with your entire family.

NOT A GOOD LIE

and now they're asking if I want to wax my lip or brow. Um, no? I don't have a mustache . . . crap, do I have a mustache? No, they're just trying to upsell. But shoot. My bikini line. Do I even want to go there? Is it presumptuous to think things will go that far tonight with Jeff_Austin2Brooklyn? I don't want to be that kind of girl. On the other hand, I *am* that kind of girl—let's be real—and I don't want to look like an Amazon rain forest down there. Okay. I will get a new razor and do some emergency maintenance at home. I don't want it to seem like I KNEW I was going to end up with my pants off, so shaving my pubes will have to be good enough.

SIGNS YOUR RELATIONSHIP IS TOO ONLINE

Your favorite thing about him: he types 78wpm

You autocomplete each other's sentences

Your iPhone background is a chat room

Your first date was a hashtag

You've been on Catfish twice and still haven't met

You make dinner, he clears his cookies

You exchange GIFs at Christmas

Most of your fights are solved by rebooting

Okay. Outfit: check. Pedicure: check. Grooming: I have razor burn, but check. Hair: it's not doing what I want, but check. Makeup: check. Alright. Now I guess I just wait around for an hour or so 'til I get the text. I should probably look over Jeff_Austin2Brooklyn's profile again so I remember what he's into. Music. Cool—I like music. Vietnamese sandwiches and bubble tea—I love Vietnamese sandwiches and bubble tea! Camping? Oh man. I don't remember seeing that before. That is definitely going to be a problem since I would rather kill myself than go camping, but we can cross that bridge when we come to it.

9:10. No text. I am starting to get a little anxious but it's cool. I am a cool and understanding person. He is probably just wrapping up with his good buddies.

9:15. Maybe I didn't hear my phone? Nope. Nothing. Alright. Fine.

9:18. Okay. It's getting a little late. I hope everything is okay with him.

9:20. He probably met a girl at whatever bar he has been hanging out at and now he is bailing on our date because he has found the love of his life in a normal way that didn't involve meeting strangers on the Internet.

9:23. He definitely met someone. What an asshole. Why are guys such assholes?? Screw this dude!

9:24. Maybe I should check to see if he wrote me a message through the dating website.

9:26. Nothing on the dating site. No text. FML. I am going to write him a message and tell him off for standing me up.

9:28. DING. "Hey Brooke it's Jeff. Just left that get together. Headed to Skylark if you want to meet for a drink still."

I meet Jeff at the bar. He is cute but definitely does not have the chiseled body type I imagined based on his profile and his haircut is a little nutso. At least he's not wearing Vibrams. We have two drinks. The conversation starts out strong and then fizzles, since we already know so much from stalking one another's profiles. It's getting late, there are no sparks flying and I feel like an idiot for buying a new outfit and shaving my pubes. We have an awkward goodbye hug and that's that.

All of that build up . . . and nothing. I head home feeling a little let down. I decide to throw in the towel and just date a pint of frozen yogurt for the rest of my life. Then "PING" I get a new notification that I have a message from the dating site. A guy named Charles_In_Charge has sent me a message! I go to bed excited and convinced that THIS date will be the one . . .

The Takeaway:
The Girl Code to online dating is that you have to be a warrior because it's tough out in those streets! Emotional armor is a must and maybe even some smoke bombs if you're caught in a bad date and need to leave ASAP! In the dating game you win some and you lose some and that's perfectly fine—but, girl, you have to put yourself out there if you're going to find out, right?

All of my Internet dates have ended one of four ways:

1 I got a little too tipsy, hooked up with the guy and then never heard from him again.

2 I really believed we had hit it off and was convinced there would be a second date . . . and then never heard from him again.

3 The date was fun but there wasn't a lot of chemistry, so I ended up with a new Friend Zone buddy.

4 Actual chemistry, led to an actual second date. Boom.

Esther Ku

If you're going to make an online profile, you should try to make it a little mysterious. Don't tell everything about yourself or you'll have nothing to talk about.

THE MYSTERIOUS
ESTER KU

RELIGIOUS VIEWS:	TELL YOU LATER
POLITICAL VIEWS:	TLL U L8R
GENDER:	TTYL

Alice Wetterlund

You can be Jewish and go to JDate. Or you can be poor and go to OKCupid. Or you can be an old sea captain and there's a site for that. And cat lovers, too.

OLD SEA CAPTAIN

STEER YOUR NAUTICAL VESSEL

CAT LOVERS

Some dates are gonna go badly. At least you'll have some hilarious stories to tell your girlfriends at happy hour. On the other hand, tons of people have met their future husbands on the World Wide Web. Everything else in between is a fun excuse to put on a cute outfit, meet dudes, get some and be your charming self. Anything is possible in Internet dating land. So log on, take a cute selfie, and wink at that cute guy named Hot_Dawg_Vendor86.

GirlCode:

WHEN IN DOUBT, REBOOT.

Bad Boys

Laura Murphy

You just have to know how to distinguish the crappy dude who will forget to call you until he needs bail money, from the hardened man who will grab your hair while kissing you and tenderly whisper his tortured secrets into your ear.

Carly Aquilino

A bad boy is a guy that you know is no good for you, but you still date him anyway.

 ou know what they say: burn me once, shame on you . . . burn me twice, I will have sex with you forever. Okay, they don't really say that. But when it comes to bad boys, they should. We've all been there. Waiting for a call from the hot guy of few words who disappears randomly, maybe because he got arrested or maybe because he is off rumbling in the streets (if it's the fifties). We get tingly every time he mumbles our name and flips his head to get his hair out of his eyes.

Bad boys are like a drug that we can't get enough of. Sometimes that drug comes in the form of a scruffy, brooding loner who drifts into and out of your life, or sometimes it's just a loser with a poor grasp of the English language, who steals stuff from a 7-11 while posing as a brooding loner. Stay away from the shoplifting poser types. At worst they turn into criminals, at best they are shitty boyfriends.

The benchmark of bad boys is the rare and elusive rebel with a cause; the bad boy who lives by a code, who only does bad against bad and builds protective walls around himself that only the love of the right woman can break down. You know, like Wolverine. Although they mainly inhabit movies and cable TV series, it doesn't mean we shouldn't hold out hope that they exist in real life. You just have to know how to distinguish the crappy dude who will forget to call you until he needs bail money, from the hardened man who will grab your hair while kissing you and tenderly whisper his tortured secrets into your ear.

MOM'S BAD BOY METER

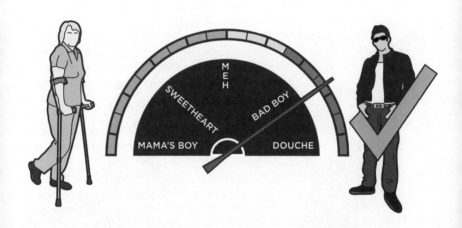

 *April Rose*

The best way to test if your guy's a bad boy is introduce him to your mom. If your mom doesn't like him, he's a bad boy.

Jessimae Peluso

What makes bad boys attractive is the fact that you're going to have some hot sex. Regular guys do missionary. Bad boys, you're Cirque De Soleil.

REGULAR SEX   **BAD BOY SEX**

I speak from experience when I say it's really not that hard to figure out which one is which and to stay away from the lame one. Like a lot of our struggles as girls, it comes down to acknowledging the reality of a situation as opposed to talking ourselves into believing what we want to believe. So yeah, it's easy to figure out . . . but hard as hell to actually execute.

I once lost a couple of months in a bad boy vortex. He was a mall security guard. I know what you are thinking, how can an authority figure empowered with protecting and serving a Piercing Pagoda, several electronics stores, and the multiplex cinema be bad? Well, consider this: he was older, mysterious about his past, he had a weapon (okay it was a flashlight, but it was heavy), he didn't seem to give a shit about his job, and he would lavish me with attention then disappear for days. Plus he had a girlfriend who worked in Customer Service. Told you. Bad boy.

Carly Aquilino

Girls get into relationships with bad boys because they think they can change them. But, at the end of the day, you cant remove a face tattoo.

I was in love. He would show up late at night at my job, take me somewhere secluded and unwrap me like candy, whispering things about how sweet I smelled. I was so drunk on his bad boyness that all of his sugary metaphors made me weak in the knees. How could someone so evasive and dark be so poetic? The reality was I worked at a candy store in the mall. Of course I smelled sweet, I was slinging Sour Patch Kids for five hours every day after school. He was literally just looking at things around me and making up sentences about them to get in my pants. I got wise to this after about three months, but I didn't want to let go of the fantasy. So I quieted my voice of reason with malted milk balls and went on breaking all sorts of Girl Code.

Jamie Lee

They can just win you by squinting.
You see them across the room and you're like,
"I have to go. I have to be with this person."
It's like a sexy alien abduction.

BAD BOY ALIEN ABDUCTION

Some nights he would sneak me into late movies and tell me how hot it was that I was his secret. If he sensed I was pulling away from him at all, he would wax on about how hardened he had become and how I was the only one who made him feel anything anymore. That should have been a massive red flag. Real bad boys with tough exteriors don't talk about their tough exteriors. They just stand and squint a little, as if their tortured soul is a burden they must silently shoulder alone until they find the right woman to share it with. Although near-sighted guys do the same thing when they need glasses so make sure it is the right kind of squint.

It got to the point where I would picture myself ending it dramatically in the Food Court while his Customer Service girlfriend looked on from her kiosk next door, dramatically calling him out for being a two-timer masquerading as a bad boy, using his perfectly fitted uniform to take advantage of naïve mall employees. But then the next day he would wink at me while I was drowning my self-loathing in Taco Bell and I would forget the whole breakup idea and end up back in the secret hallway behind Abercrombie letting him lick mild sauce off my neck. That's another thing to watch out for . . . bad boys with a code don't eat Food Court food. In fact, I am not sure if they eat at all. They drink. But they may not eat.

My foray into faux bad boy territory finally blew up when I quit my job at the candy store for a sweet gig at the movie theater. See I had always worked on the second floor of the mall. Customer Service was on the first floor. So I could conveniently ignore the fact that I was really just the other woman. I use the term "woman" loosely because I was in college and still sleeping in a twin bed, but you know what I mean. I have to give the guy some credit, too. Most affairs take place in neighboring cities or at least a couple of blocks away. He was juggling two girls separated only by an escalator. But again, there's nothing really "bad" about that, it's more just lazy.

SHELF-LIFE OF A BAD BOY

HOT 'N' FRESH

LOOKS FINE

Shalyah Evans

Bad boys grow up into jerks.
Well, they're already jerks, they're just going to be old and less cute, so it's not so endearing.

Once I started at the movie theater, I had to work in the ticket booth on the first floor, right down the hall from Customer Service. The first day he saw me in my red vest at my new post, he walked into a column, literally. Then bee-lined it to his real girlfriend and made out with her in front of me. Point taken. I ran to the bathroom and threw up curly fries, then went home sick. There was no denying it now. He wasn't a bad boy. He wasn't even cool. The guy was just an asshole. When I went back to work later that week, it was as if a fog had cleared. Suddenly, I realized he wasn't even that hot. His hair was a bit weird and his squinty faces were the wrong kind, which also made me worried about my security at the mall. I also realized there was nobody to blame but myself. He might have sold me a headline, but I filled in the rest of the story and convinced myself it was real.

SMELLS FUNNY   GETTING OLD   EXPIRED

I am not saying the perfect bad boy doesn't exist. He might be out there somewhere and you might be the one to find him and tame him. Just keep a couple things in mind on your quest. Bad boys with a code break rules for a reason, not just because they don't give a shit about authority. And the rules they break aren't the ones relating to things like fidelity, honesty or relationships. Also, stealing stuff is not hot-bad, it's just bad-bad, even if all they're stealing is someone else's material. Anyone poetic who doesn't seem like they should be, probably isn't poetic at all. If they aren't plagiarizing then you are most likely giving them way more credit that they deserve. (Musicians might be the loophole to this rule, but they come with their own set of issues.)

Nessa
~

Get all the bad boy in you out. Have crazy sex with bad boys, get it out of your system, learn some new tricks. But marry the good guy.

OTHER THINGS BAD BOYS ARE BAD AT

Annunciating	Good posture
Showering on the reg	Tucking in shirts
Acknowledging it when you sneeze	Obeying traffic laws
Timely text replies	Punctuality
	Ironing

The Girl Code to bad boys is: don't settle for anything less than the real thing, if you can find it. Accept now that the only poems you will get will be from the quiet nerd who paid attention in English or the guy who's majoring in Literature and always wants to give you backrubs. Those guys are real, easy to find, and they probably won't get arrested. There are worse things than a shoulder rub here and there. So until you find a real life Wolverine, maybe give those guys a shot and stay away from all the wannabe criminal and loser bad boys loitering around the Food Court. You know what? When it comes to dating, maybe just stay away from the mall altogether. That's Girl Code.

GirlCode:

GOOD BAD IS HARD TO FIND.

Being Slutty

Sachi Ezura

**Nothing helps you find yourself
quite like abandoning all your sexual hang-ups
and just going for it.**

Carly Aquilino

You know you're a slut if you have a slutty nickname. I went to high school with a girl named Patty Blowjobs and another girl named Jenny Handjobs.

 t is in every girl's best interest to go through a slutty phase. I'm not talking about being gross—use protection, only do what makes you feel comfortable, don't be a dummy. Nothing helps you find yourself quite like abandoning all your sexual hang-ups and just going for it. I have far too many friends who are going to end up somebody's wife before they ever let themselves go a little crazy. Life is short. Give yourself a good year or two to get your Ke$ha on. Then you can go back to being Kelly Clarkson or Katie Couric.

A slutty phase is the ultimate way to prove to yourself exactly what you've got going on. You put on a pair of stripper heels, work that body on the dance floor, and realize for the first time in your life, that if you want to be having sex, you can be having sex. Every fully-formed woman deserves to know that she has the power to make shit happen tonight. Unfortunately, the ratio of sluttiness to self-esteem is a bell curve. A six month slutty phase can teach you that you're a hot piece of ass, but any longer than that and you may start feeling like just a piece of ass. We're aiming for sex goddess here, not sex worker.

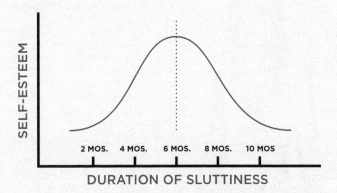

SELF-ESTEEM

2 MOS. 4 MOS. 6 MOS. 8 MOS. 10 MOS

DURATION OF SLUTTINESS

There are three ideal times to go through said slutty phase. Lucky for you, dear reader, I have done all three and emerged a smarter, more worldly woman.

Right Before You Graduate: Before I left for college, I made friends with my first slut. A slutty friend is a lovely thing to have. They have the best stories and are ballsy enough to get you to do things you wouldn't otherwise do. And no matter how silly you let yourself get, they will always be ten times worse.

In our last weeks of high school, she encouraged me to make a list of ten guys I wanted to make out with before I graduated. I managed to knock out seven of them on schedule and two more over the summer. I was still a virgin and never let it get past boob grabbage. I guess that made me the worst kind of slut—the prude slut. It is tremendous fun to be a prude slut as a teenage girl, especially if you enjoy attention and the sound of male whining. However, you have to understand that you are causing men physical pain. You are leading them towards climax, then deserting them halfway around the bases. Or, in my case, just making out with a bunch of gay theater dudes.

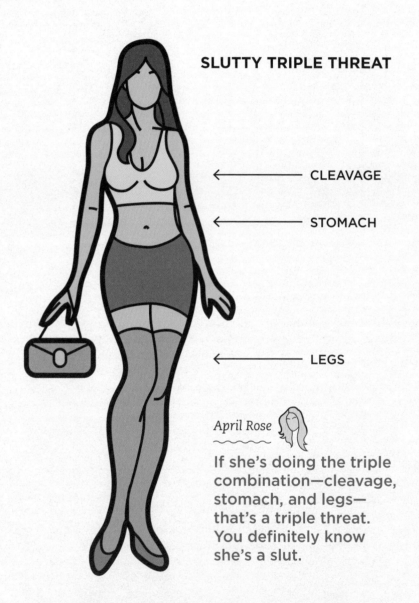

SLUTTY TRIPLE THREAT

← CLEAVAGE

← STOMACH

← LEGS

April Rose

If she's doing the triple combination—cleavage, stomach, and legs— that's a triple threat. You definitely know she's a slut.

When I got to college, I met a new group of people who knew nothing of my lascivious list. I was all like, "I'm not very experienced," and my new classmates took me at my word. Take advantage of the moment before you reinvent yourself to make a few mistakes. You're about to wipe your slate clean, so go ahead and get that slate dirty. Slate it up.

On Vacation: That summer between high school and college, I went on vacation with my mom to the Dominican Republic. It was there I met Alexa, a dork like me who had experienced a similar sexual awakening her senior spring. Together we decided to make our trip one for the ages by putting the moves on anyone with a resort bracelet and a tan. We developed all kinds of plans and schemes to make out with guys on the dance floor, but we found that we didn't need those plans and schemes. All we had to say was, "Do you want to make out?" This was a stunning revelation, which led to a debauched week of dance-floor grinding sessions and poolside tonsil hockey.

Vacation sluttery is even better than pre-graduation sluttery because you won't see any of these people ever again. If you slut it up at college, you could end up running into Mr. One Night Stand at some horrible alumni event. But lucky for me, there's no such thing as a Club Med ten-year reunion.

Right After A Breakup: This is the most liberating one because you are SO SAD. You are letting loose in an effort to make yourself feel better. Your self-esteem has been destroyed and all you want is someone to touch your hair and tell you you're pretty. Get your friends to convince you to wipe your face off and put on a sexy dress and then go out on the town and be aggressively slutty. Being heartbroken is a great time to take risks, because it literally can't get any worse. Soon enough, you're going to be in a relationship again and you're going to lose the opportunity to find the hottest, dumbest boy in the bar and bang his nonexistent brains out.

Now, I know what you're thinking—none of these are really that slutty. I know a real slut, and that's not a real slut. A real slut has sex with a hundred guys. A real slut lets guys finger her on the school bus or goes down on entire teams or fraternities. A real slut breaks some rule that you've decided you are never, ever going to break, no matter how much tequila you drink. But I'm going to let you in on a little secret. There's no such thing as a slut. Not in the real sense of the word anyway. "Slut," along with its tamer but ruder cousin "bitch" are words designed to keep you from going after what you want and having fun. You can be the kind of girl who kisses a lot of dudes—or kisses a lot of dudes and girls, or has sex with a lot of dudes, or has weird kinky sex with one dude—and still remain A GOOD PERSON. Remind yourself of that. Your sexual choices do not dictate who you are as a person. You can do whatever you want to do.

That being said, you don't want to be a girl who is callous with her own heart and body. Feel free to go out there and try some crazy stuff, but there are a few guidelines you should probably follow for your own sake:

1 Use protection.
The last thing anyone likes is a pregnant slut with HPV.

2 If you're doing it to make people like you, guess what?
They probably won't in the morning.

3 Know that guys will talk.
If you hook up with multiple guys in one fraternity, group of friends, or amateur bird-watching league, it won't be long before they start comparing notes on your awkward sex noises and mismatched nipples.

4 Don't hook up with guys in a club if you don't know they're single.
Unless you like getting your weave pulled out on the dance floor.

5 Stay out of your own wading pool.
You don't want to end up at a party looking around thinking, I've slept with everyone here.

6 Don't hook up with your friends' boyfriends or exes.

7 Don't get into a weird van with a stranger.

Alice Wetterlund

My favorite slut is the divorcée. It almost makes me want to get a divorce, so that I can get a pool, and then just a succession of pool cleaners—hotter each time.

DIVORCED ALICE

THE DRUNK SLUT

Jamie Lee

My favorite slut is the drunk slut, because she's the classic. She's the Chevy convertible of sluts. She's durable, reliable, sturdy, and always has her top down.

ESSENTIAL ITEMS FOR SLUTS

An ice breaker	Phone charger
A healthy interest in penises	Couple of jokes
Breath Right nasal strips	Cab fare
Dance moves	Eyepatch
Condoms	(great disguise for getting out of there)

That's pretty much it. Otherwise, do whatever you want. No matter how deep a hole you dig yourself into, you'll probably be able to get out of it and be somebody's wife someday. So have fun while you're young! One day when you're forty, climbing into bed with the husband you've cherished for years, you can remember the time you had sex in a coat closet with an Italian and smile. Too bad you never found out his name.

GirlCode:

IT'S COLLEGE FOR YOUR BOD.

STDs

Chelsea White

We have to honor Girl Code by not letting our nerves stand in the way of keeping our vaginas as safe as possible.

Jessimae Peluso

You have one coochie kingdom. If you don't do everything to keep it clean, you should be a dude.

 can't think of many things that suck more than getting sick from having sex. Sexually transmitted diseases take something that's the best and make it the absolute worst. Like a birthday cake that punches you in the face.

Girl Code for STDs is straightforward: DON'T GET ONE. But crossing our fingers every time we uncross our legs isn't going to cut it. We need to be as proactive about protecting of our vaginas as we are about keeping our other valuables safe. So why is it that we'll huddle under an overhang for hours to save our favorite strappy wedges from a sudden downpour, but in a sudden torrent of passion we sometimes neglect to show our vaginas the same consideration?

Probably because the stuff we gotta do to keep our vaginas safe can be awkward as hell! When it comes to STDs, we can't get hung up feeling nervous about dotting our i's and crossing our t's (or protecting our v's and inspecting guys' p's, as it were). What we should be nervous about is what could happen if we DON'T! But remembering this in the moment is easier said than done.

The key to upholding Girl Code is a two-part process. First, learn and love the Vagina Safety Steps. These are non-negotiable rules that will keep you STD-free. Second, have a Psych Up Strategy to power you through each step.

STD STAGES

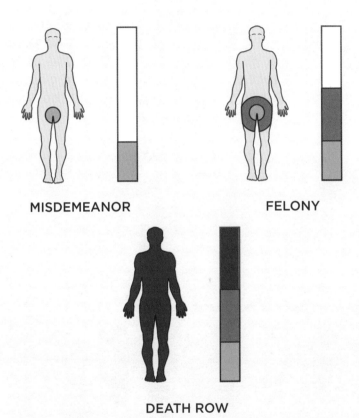

MISDEMEANOR

FELONY

DEATH ROW

April Rose

There are different stages of STDs.
A misdemeanor is like crabs or chlamydia.
A Felony is like herpes or warts. And then
there's death row—you know what that is.

 *Carly Aquilino*

Depending on how slutty you are, is how often you should get checked for STDs. If you're hooking up with a few guys every once in a while, you can get checked every six months. But if you're going out and hooking up with different guys all the time, you should get checked every day.

DR. CARLY SAYS:

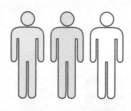

SIX MONTHS

EVERY DAY

Vagina Safety Step One: Get Tested. Getting an STD test for the first time can be nerve-racking. Truth be told, getting one for the one-hundredth time is nerve-racking! Waiting for the results seems like an eternity, whether you have reason to believe you have an STD or not. I got tested before I was even sexually active because I was convinced I had somehow contracted herpes through osmosis. *(How do we KNOW that it can't be caught through denim?!)* It turned out my "herpes" was just an ingrown hair, but the relief I felt from knowing trumped all nerves leading up to and during the event.

Psych Up Strategy: Now, any time I'm creeped out about getting tested, I remind myself that NOT knowing is what I should be nervous about. Not only will the wondering drive me bananas, but every day I'm in the dark is a day I could inadvertently become "That Chic Who Gave Kevin The Clap." I mean, if the stuff that can happen inside our crotches was happening on our faces we would RUN to the doctor, right?

Vagina Safety Step Two: Talk to Your Doc. I used to feel super weird talking to my gyno about the stuff that was going on down there. I figured she would either think I was a nut for worrying about every little imperfection and irregularity or that the truths about my sex life would scandalize her. I'd feed her half-truths ("Well, we're not NOT monogamous.") or flat out lie ("I've never even seen a condom-less penis!"), until I finally realized that I WAS a nut for worrying about what she would think and compromising my vagina in the process.

Psych Up Strategy: Trust that gynos everywhere have seen and heard it all. We could not shock them if we tried. For every case of razor burn we run by them, someone else has walked in with a kazoo stuck in her cooch. The next time you're panicky just think about the scenario from your doc's perspective:
YOU: *"Hello Doctor, I would like you to check my vagina for sexually transmitted diseases because I am sexually active."*
DOC: *"Fantastic! You are such a responsible, admirable young lady to be proactive about your health and the health of your sexual partners. Kudos to you. In fact, here is a Kudos bar as a reward for your good decisions."*

See? Doc loves you for your forthrightness. She even gave you a granola bar! So when you're in that gyno gown feeling uncomfortable about being honest, think about how much more uncomfortable you would be with herpes.

Vagina Safety Step Three: Share STD Stats. This may be the most nerve-racking part of staying STD-free because it's never any easy convo to kick off. I'd rather talk about diarrhea than gonorrhea. But letting a guy slide by without an STD test talk is a major breach of Girl Code.

Nessa

If you feel like you have something weird—something itches, burns, looks odd, bumpy, any of that—go to the clinic and get it checked out.

CHECK FOR SIGNS

Psych Up Strategy: I always remind myself of what the flip side sounds like: "Yeah, I got genital warts because I didn't want to make things awkward." Listen, we'd never hesitate to question a guy's music preferences, hygiene routine, or stance on the war between LOL and hahaha, so why be nervous about asking him the most important question of all? A great way to break the ice is to offer up your stats: "So I just wanted you to know that I was tested last month and I'm good to go! How about you?" Just keep it casual and he'll feel weird NOT replying back as confidently as you.

Vagina Safety Step Four: Thou Shalt Always Use Condoms! This is the most important Safety Step of all. Yes, condoms can be a pain. They're like that friend who has the best of intentions, but annoys the crap out of you. But they are also the reason we can get some and not get sick. Remember: Even if you diligently followed Step Three and he claims to be clean, you can never know for sure.

Psych Up Strategy: There likely isn't a lady amongst us who hasn't heard, "It just feels better without one," right? When a guy feeds me lines like that, I love to feed them right back: "Well your options are having sex with a condom or not having sex, so let me know your preference. Because I'm cool to just stop and grab a snack instead." Given a choice between sex and no sex, guys will ALWAYS choose sex.

And we can't leave it up to guys to be the contraception keepers. Stick a few condoms in your purse right next to your other necessities because pants-less is no place to be when you realize neither of you is packing. I also find that keeping a parenting magazine bedside inspires them to come around pretty quickly. Because you know what's even more annoying than a condom? Nursing a kid and Chlamydia at the same time.

Carly Aquilino

**The best way to avoid getting an STD is to make sure you always use protection.
And also, probably drink a lot of orange juice.
I'm not a doctor, but I think that it can't hurt.**

**BROUGHT TO YOU BY
CITRUS FARMERS OF AMERICA**

Carly Aquilino

I always thought that STD stood for "Something to Drink." But now I realize that STD stands for Sexually Transmitted Disease. Either way, I'll always have one.

STDs are not shameful or whorey—but they are a reality no matter how many sexual partners we've had. We have to honor Girl Code by not letting our nerves stand in the way of keeping our vaginas as safe as possible. Just like our strappy wedges, they're counting on us! After all, we only get one. No swapsies, no take-backs. It's YOUR vagina, so never let anyone make you feel silly for looking out for it. Those people don't have to live with syphilis, you do. It's like that talking trench coat dog always said: "Only YOU can prevent crotch fires." Maybe I'm paraphrasing, but you get the point. Vagina Code!

GirlCode:

THE VAGINA YOU SAVE JUST MIGHT BE YOUR OWN.

Penises

Wenonah Hoye

The penis is a real life magic wand.

Melanie Iglesias

The first time you see one, you think, "Ugh, that's a penis. I don't know how I feel about penises." Until you *feel* the penis.

Every little girl dreams that some day she will fall in love with a handsome prince. But what you don't read in fairytales is this: every prince has a penis. And once you're old enough to understand what he uses that penis for and where he wants you to put it, it kind of complicates the whole Knight in Shining Armor fantasy. What I've learned is that the penis is a real life magic wand. And if the man who wields it knows what he's doing, this wand has the power to transform you into a princess and transport you to Happily Ever After.

The first time I ever felt a penis, I was thirteen and both terrified and curious about what boys had in their pants. I knew a lot of the dirty words for it and I had a girlfriend who had even touched one, but beyond that they were a complete mystery to me. I had been flirting all summer with an older boy I had met at a YMCA camp. He had a reputation as a bad boy with a lot of experience. A big bad wolf, who my friends warned would try to feel me up or finger me. I followed him into the deep dark woods anyway. I let him put his hand up my shirt and when he lay on top of me I felt something hard press into my thigh. My heart stopped. Should I touch it? If I don't touch it, will he still like me? If I *do* touch it will he think I'm a slut? I held my breath and slowly moved my hand down towards his crotch. Before I got there he let out a little moan. His body tensed, then relaxed, and he rolled off of me. I had no idea what had just happened, but apparently we were done. As we walked back to camp in awkward silence, I wondered why there was a damp patch on my shorts.

PINK TORPEDO

BANANA

After that I was a bit wary of sheep in wolves' clothing, and it wasn't until I was fifteen and had my first real boyfriend that I tried to touch a penis again. I had absolutely no idea what to do with it, but I'd seen enough R-rated movies to know that some kind of up and down motion was a step in the right direction. I was amazed that something so soft could get so hard. And it was the strangest looking thing. Thick and veiny, it pointed straight up—like a pink torpedo. That was the first penis I ever had inside me and, although I loved the boy it came with, it always kind of felt like riding a bicycle without a seat—it got me where I wanted to go, but I usually felt a little sore afterward.

Nessa
~~~

If you've never seen a penis, I'm telling you now, it's going to freak you out. You're gonna first feel around. You're like, "Oh, this is cool." Then the minute you look at it—make eye contact—it just changes your life.

UNFORTUNATE FAIRY TALE RESEMBLANCES

LITTLE RED RIDING HOOD

THE BIG BAD WOLF

In college I learned that not all penises are created equal. There was one that looked kind of like a hot dog (and not the fat ballpark kind, but the skinny, anemic-looking ones from the carts that you know you shouldn't eat 'cause they've been sitting in that nasty grey water all day). It was so small and skinny, that when he got on top of me I couldn't even feel if he'd put it in or not. Yes, size matters. But also width, shape, feel, and taste. The variations are infinite. Some are straight. Some lean to the left or right. Each one is as unique as a snowflake. And it's different for each woman what feels best. It can even depend on what we're looking for at a given time in our sexual lives. I mean, sometimes Beauty wants a Prince and sometimes she wants the Beast.

A semester in London taught me that English penises come with little hoodies. When soft, the uncircumcised foreskin covers the whole thing. But once it gets hard, out pops a little turtle head to say hello. Apparently, all that extra skin

Carly Aquilino

Penises are so disgusting. But we still love them. It's like exactly what a man is to us.

TOM THUMB

UGLY DUCKLING

RIP VAN WRINKLE

increases sensitivity, which is great for the guy, but you better wash that thing if you want me to put it in my mouth.

In my twenties, I stopped looking for Prince Charming when I met a Sorcerer with exceptional wand skills. His tool curved a little at the middle like a banana and the tip was a perfect mushroom cap with a little winking eye in the center. It was love at first sight. The weight of it felt so right in my hands that it brought me to my knees (literally). And when he put it inside me, it hit this spot that I hadn't even known was there. I felt like Goldilocks with baby bear's porridge: this one was just right.

Jessimae Peluso

Does size matter? Anybody who says it doesn't is a lying slob. My vagina is a room. And if your dick doesn't fill it, emotionally and physically, we can't go to IKEA and buy a shelf to put in there to fill up the space. I'm going to fuck your brother.

PRINCE CHARMING

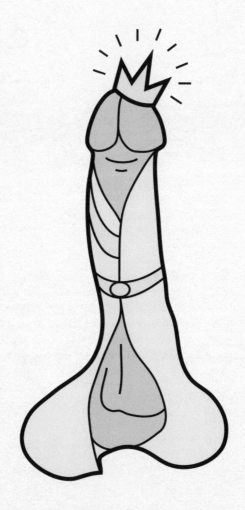

WHEN BIG IS TOO BIG

You can only photograph
it in panorama

Every time you ride it,
PETA protests

You can take it all the way,
but there's a layover in Dallas

It's censored by Google Maps

Scientists are unsure
how to stop it

It does something to the WiFi

Every erection flattens Tokyo

Shalyah Evans

I guess size matters to me in that I don't want to be questioning whether or not I'm having sex and I don't want to be in pain.

I'm all for fairytales, but now that I'm a big girl I've learned that a lot of the time Mr. Right is really just Mr. Right Now. And that's okay, because each experience teaches you something new about what you like and what you don't like. Knowing what's right for you and finding the prince who knows how to give it to you is critical in the pursuit of sexual pleasure. It's up to us to figure that out and sometimes you gotta kiss a lot of frogs before you find your perfect penis. Girl Code.

GirlCode:

LIKE A GLASS SLIPPER, ONLY MADE OF PENIS.

Friends with Benefits

Sachi Ezura

A good FWB is like the shitty Chinese place on your block. Sure, it wasn't your first choice of food but it's open past midnight and it tastes great when you're drunk.

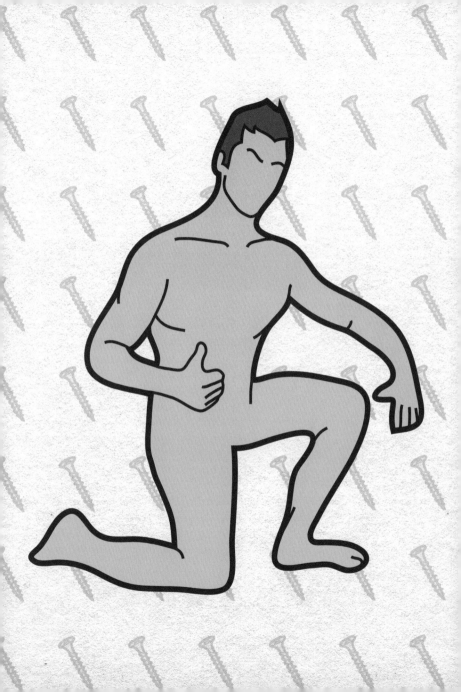

Jessimae Peluso

The only way to have a successful friends with benefits situation: keep your heart closed, and your legs open. Like a lady.

he summer before I went to college, I had the biggest crush on my friend Max. To be honest, I had only befriended him in high school because I thought he was cute. But I soon figured out that underneath THE HOTTEST BODY I'VE EVER SEEN ON A SEVENTEEN-YEAR-OLD BOY (note: this was before Taylor Lautner), there was a guy who was a pretty great hang. One night after way too many drinks (two and a half Smirnoff Ices, to be precise), I decided to make a move. After all, I was leaving for college in a couple weeks. Why the hell not?

Unsurprisingly, Max was into the idea of becoming friends with benefits. At the time, I was all like "Really? For serious? You're down to do fun naked stuff together with zero boyfriend responsibilities??? This is nuts." In retrospect, I realize he was a seventeen-year-old boy who was clearly on the winning side of the deal. I'd sneak into his parents' house at all hours of the night and we'd watch DVDs and eat leftovers and then get to the fun stuff. And at the end of the summer, I didn't want it to end.

CATCH OF THE DAY

 *Jessimae Peluso*

The worst part of friends with benefits is catching feelings. Or an STD. Or both.

I didn't think I wanted him to be my boyfriend. After all, we were going off to college soon and I had always imagined myself in a serious relationship with a shy guitar-playing cutie rather than the captain of the basketball team. But I knew when we went off to college, he'd be swamped with slutty co-eds putting their grubby little hands all over him. I didn't want to picture it. I just wanted him to keep putting his grubby little hands on me and only me. In the words of Hannah Horvath from *Girls*—a true Girl Code hero—"I don't even want a boyfriend. I just want someone who wants to hang out all the time, and thinks I'm the best person in the world, and wants to have sex with only me."

As a slightly more well-adjusted twentysomething, I have had a couple of successful 'friends with benefits' relationships. But it is not easy. Chances are one of you is going to want to turn it into something more. And it's only fun and carefree and convenient until it isn't. Here you are, thinking you've conquered commitment-free sex and then all of a sudden, one of you turns into a sad ball of feelings, crying in the corner of a party—and let's hope to God it's him.

But if you can make it work, if you can truly figure out how to remain detached and drama-free, having a friend with benefits is THE BEST. A good FWB is like the shitty Chinese place on your block. Sure, it wasn't your first choice of food but it's open past midnight and it tastes great when you're drunk. Between my last serious relationship and my current boyfriend, I had a dude on speed dial who was there whenever I needed him. Let's call him Plan B. He didn't care if I was wearing my cute underwear. I didn't have to put on makeup or suffer through small talk. Hell, he didn't even care if I'd showered. After all, we were buds. Buds who boned. If I had had a shitty date or got bored watching *Friday Night Lights* with my cat, Plan B was ready with an erection and a smile. And when I started dating my current boyfriend, Plan B was just as chill reverting back to semi-friend status.

Nicole Byer

You get two activities and you're done. And one of them has to be fucking.

SO my tried and true rules for a successful no-drama sex-buddy sitch:

1 Choose your FWB wisely.
Your FWB shouldn't be your BFF-WB. If you hook up with your best dude friend, he's probably either going to become your one true love or the guy you have to avoid at parties for the rest of your life. So choose someone who you wouldn't mind cutting out of your life if things go south. And for God's sake, no matter how good the sex was, never ever use your ex-boyfriend as a friend with benefits. I'm having a panic attack just thinking about that shitshow.

2 Keep things light.
Save the intense heart-to-hearts and sob sessions for your next boyfriend. The only question your FWB needs to answer is "Do you have a condom?"

3 He's using you. Use him back.
An FWB is like a vibrator with a convenient man-body attached. Think of your no-strings-attached sex sessions as preparation for all of the amazing strings-attached sex you're going to have in the future. You can try things you wouldn't try with a third date or a serious boyfriend. Always wanted to be tied up? Or show up at someone's door dressed as a schoolgirl? This is the perfect opportunity to attempt your *Fifty Shades of Grey* fantasy. If he gets weirded out, in the words of the great Jay-Z, on to the next one.

4 Don't ask, don't tell.
Whatever he's doing when you're not there is none of your business. Every time you get the urge to ask him about his date last night or whose pink razor is in his shower, remind yourself that you don't really want to know. You're both still single. Luckily, this means what you're doing isn't his business either. So get out there. Live yo life. Strut yo stuff. YOLO

5 This is what you signed up for.
If you find yourself getting caught up in movies like *No Strings Attached* and *Friends with Benefits*, you're doing it wrong. Those are fantasies. In real life, if you tell a guy "I don't want to be your girlfriend. I just want to screw around," he is going to listen to you. And he is going to be really confused when you

HOW TO KNOW WHEN IT'S OVER

HIM   YOU

 *Carly Aquilino*

You know that a friend with benefits is over when he gets a girlfriend and you're crying on your couch into a pint of Ben and Jerry's.

start freaking out because the TGIFriday's waitress gave him her number. So don't. That's not what he's there for. If your heart is saying "I want him" more than your snatch, you're getting too attached.

That last rule is probably the most important one, and the one I failed to follow with Max. At the end of the summer, we both went off to college. We continued to text and gchat and every time he'd mention the girls he was seeing and how much fun he was having at school, I'd get jealous and weird. When we came home for Thanksgiving break, I put my tried-and-true moves on him, did the dirty, then went straight into Crazy Girl Mode and tearfully asked him why he wouldn't be my boyfriend.

What he told me then stuck with me through my next decade of dysfunctional dating. "You can't trick someone into being your boyfriend," he said. WHY THE FUCK NOT? I thought. I had done everything right. I had been easy-going and fun and a genuine down-ass chick. But he had told me from the start that he didn't want a girlfriend. And somewhere, buried deep in my subconscious under all the layers of not wanting a boyfriend—or at least saying I didn't want a boyfriend—I had been playing a long con. I had thought if I just stayed the course, he'd eventually change his mind. To this day, any time my girl friends get into a casual situation with a guy they really like, I remind them, "You can't trick this guy into being your boyfriend." And most of the time, they still try.

The fact of the matter is, if a guy wants to be your boyfriend, he'll make it clear to you. No guy ever just ends up as someone's boyfriend without noticing. So use that FWB for everything they're good for and then move on. Shitty Chinese is delicious, but if you eat it every night, you're never going to see what else is out there.

IDEAL FRIEND WITH BENEFITS

GPA:
1.97

MUSIC:
NICKELBACK

OCCUPATION:
ON PAROLE

BENEFITS NOT INCLUDED IN YOUR FWB PACKAGE

Dental Plan	Good grammer
Candle-lit dinners	A free scoop on your birthday
A shoulder to cry on	HBO
His facebook password	A +1 at family events
A 401k	Love
Butt stuff	

Alice Wetterlund

If you can see ten things about him that are already deal breakers, that's perfect. That's your friend with benefits.

GirlCode:

FEELINGS SOLD SEPARATELY.

Contraception

Laura Murphy

She who has the vagina, controls it all.

Carly Aquilino

Contraception is a great thing that was invented to prevent girls from getting diseases or—even worse—pregnant.

 am no statistician but I am seventy-nine percent sure that one hundred percent of us hated the first conversation we ever had about contraception. Whether it was your parents sitting you down to talk about birds, bees, and humping; your slightly sweaty health class teacher awkwardly rolling a condom onto something that shouldn't be condomized; your "cool aunt" asking if you want her to "hook you up with the pill;" or even you bringing it up moments before the first time you actually have sex, it totally sucked.

Or maybe you are the .00001% of girls who hasn't had a conversation about it yet. Maybe reading this is the first you have heard about this crazy category of devices and elixirs that, when used properly, magically prevent you from getting knocked up, inheriting something itchy and burny or, well, something contagious that lasts forever. If that's the case, please keep reading . . . and also get the Internet, or at least basic cable.

SAFE

DANGEROUS

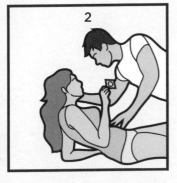

 Jessimae Peluso

You should have the contraception talk before your pants come off because it can't go the other way around. It doesn't go backwards. Why? Because that's where babies come from.

The point is that it's really hard to make talking about contraception cool. Even when it's a "cool" celebrity or "clever" advertising people delivering the message in a funny way, we all still tune out a little bit. You know why? Because they're not telling us anything we don't already know. Of course we know we should always use contraception. We're not dumb, we're the inherently smarter sex. We also know we should always wear a helmet when we ride a bike and look both ways before crossing, but I have almost been run over a hundred times by helmetless bikers I have blindly stepped in front of, so clearly we don't always do what we're supposed to. My question is: if we change the way we talk about contraception, would we all start using it more?

Nicole Byer

I'm pretty comfortable talking contraception with guys. I'm always like, "Put a condom on your dick." Guys, sleeping with me is a prize.

The following two statements are pretty much always true: NO guy likes using a condom and NO guy will say no to sex just because you insist on him wearing one. Believe me, I have heard this from a million guys (well more like a hundred guys, I don't really know a million of them). They all want to have sex. Period. They aren't going to turn it down over a condom. Of course, they won't tell you that when you're both naked and ready to go. But you can pretty much derail their argument by saying "I fucking love condoms. So if you aren't going to use one, we aren't doing it." Obviously you don't really love condoms. And yes, they will know that. But their man brains are so super charged with horny chemicals (scientific term) that they will more than likely give in.

Also, for the record, "I just want to put it in for, like, a second and then I will put one on" translates to "I think you are gullible enough to fall for this bullshit tactic." So don't. The mistake we often make in this situation is letting the guy do too much talking. We listen to whatever pitch he is making for way too long. I am not sure why because this is LITERALLY the only time we let this happen. If

HOW MEN SEE CONDOMS

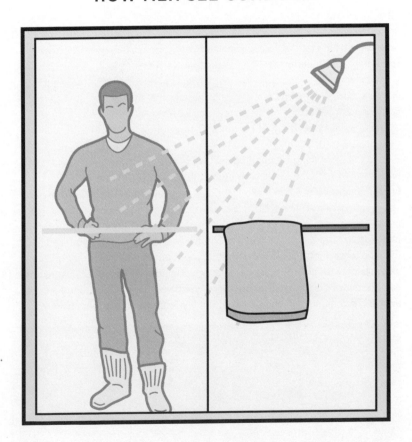

it were an argument about him looking at another girl, we wouldn't even let him get four words out without yelling at him to save his sorry-ass excuses. It might be something about the vulnerability of being naked or the crippling desire we all have to be wanted that makes us listen to his similarly sorry-ass reasons to raw dog it, but we often do, and then we have a hard time shutting him down.

Whatever reason he gives you for not wearing a condom, just know that he is using the argument because it has worked before. So if you are pretty psyched with the current state of your vajajay and you want to preserve it, just make your closing statement—feel free to be creative with it as long as it is clear—and wait while he wraps it up. In other words, change the conversation to no conversation. We are so competitive by nature, that maybe if we just started comparing notes on the funniest ways to force a guy to use a condom, we would one-up ourselves right into an STD-free zone.

Here is the other thing I learned on my own because nobody talks about it: to each her own with the whole birth control thing. The pill is great for some girls, but the hormones in it can make other girls sick, miserable, and even crazy. There are so many other options, like a birth control shot, a patch, a ring that fits snugly inside your lady parts, and some nonhormonal options such as sponges, diaphragms, and IUDs. The key is to find the one that is right for you, and to do that you have to do your homework. Ask your doctor, your slutty friend, your older sister, your friend's older sister, even your mom if she is cool. Just ask. If you do, the whole birds-bees convo can be on your terms. Then, once you learn everything you can, you should talk about it so other girls can learn from you.

THINGS NOT TO DO WHILE HE PUTS ON A CONDOM

Yawn

Check out Zappos.com

Use a bed sheet to turn yourself into a ghost

Selfie!

Time him

Slow clap

Make a call

Scream Yolo

Ask what happened on the last episode of *The Walking Dead*

 *Carly Aquilino*

I was on birth control for a month and I was a hormonal psycho. I had huge boobs, but that didn't make up for it.

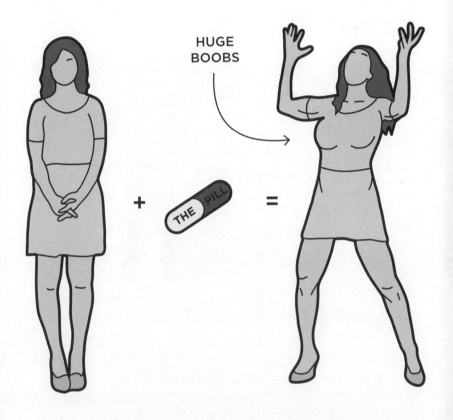

HUGE BOOBS

CARLY'S BIRTH CONTROL EQUATION

In my twenties, at the advice of my gyno, I got fitted for a diaphragm. I didn't know they even made them anymore but he thought it was a good option for me since I hate the pill but was in a monogamous relationship and didn't want to use condoms anymore. I went in blind. He showed me several sizes ranging from silver dollar pancake size to what I can only describe as mini-trampoline size. In my mind, the big one was what Courtney Love would use. I was terrified. Would I have to carry that huge thing in my purse like a latex frisbee? How embarrassing. I can't describe the relief and pride I felt the moment he told me I needed a size so small it had to be special ordered.

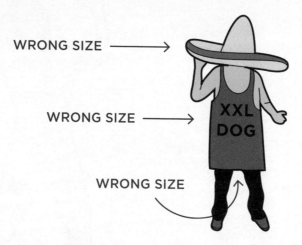

WRONG SIZE ⟶

WRONG SIZE ⟶

XXL
DOG

WRONG SIZE

Carly Aquilino

Guys with small penises who insist on wearing Magnums: don't put something on that you know is going to fall off inside of me. I don't want to have to feel around for fifteen minutes trying to find it. I'm a size seven shoe, you don't see me walking around in a size fifteen.

I spent the next two weeks bragging about how tiny my hoohah was to anyone who would listen . . . until someone pointed out that the diaphragm actually just blocks your cervical entrance and has nothing to do with vagina size. Probably should have asked someone or googled that before I announced it to everyone I knew. I will say this, though, because I had talked about it so much, when my boyfriend and I got into awkward situations with it (like the time it got stuck or the times I had to run to the bathroom to put it in), we were able to laugh about it. Talking made the whole thing more comfortable and almost fun—well, as fun as contraception can be.

The same idea applies on a grand scale as well. If we keep talking about contraception, with each other and with whoever we are banging, in our own way (instead of just being talked down to about it), we just might get better at using it. I'm not saying we are ever going to make it cool. I just mean the more we laugh at the weirdness of it, the more comfortable we'll get with the whole thing, the more other people will get comfortable with it, and then dudes won't be so shocked when we insist on a condom—and maybe the health teacher will stop dry rubbing a damn banana.

In a perfect world, we will talk and laugh about contraception so much that we will all just use it when we're supposed to and it won't even be a thing. It's been said before, but I'll say it again, the real Girl Code is: she who has the vagina, controls it all. Wield the power you got sister and demand protected perfection up in that thing.

GirlCode:

JUST USE IT.

Crushes

Wenonah Hoye

If you have reached the point where you
have the judgment and self-control of a
tweaker in a meth lab, it's time to pull back
and take stock of yourself.

Alice Wetterlund

Crushes are great. They make the world go round—otherwise Taylor Swift would not have a career.

 crush is the most intense high you can have without breaking the law. No one tells us this when we're in fourth grade and we get all breathless and excited because the boy we like talked to us at recess, but the brain is basically reacting the same way it does when it experiences its first hit of molly. In both cases the rush is so powerful, the effect on the mind and body lingers for days afterward. The crush is nature's opiate. It's free, it's legal, and most of the time it feels amazing.

Studies conducted by neuroscientists—and *Cosmo*—have shown that when you are crushing hard on a dude, the rush of chemicals that flood your brain— oxytocin, dopamine, vasopressin, and adrenaline—are similar to the types of chemicals released by narcotics like heroin and cocaine. True story. This is why there are so many similarities between the way the body reacts when it's high on drugs and the way it responds when a crush is in the same room: elevated/erratic heart rate, dry mouth, dilated pupils, impairment of rational thought and judgment, a pervasive sense of euphoria—often followed by spiraling anxiety and a creeping sense of self-doubt (they don't call it a "crush" for nothing).

NICOLE'S CRUSH TYPE

(CHEESE) $\longrightarrow$

Nicole Byer

My crush type is white, pasty, chubby, and close to death. The more un-healthy you look, the happier I am. If you look like you drink Velveeta cheese, I'm attracted to you and I don't know why.

This parallel also explains why we have a tendency to make asses of ourselves in front of the object of our affection. Who hasn't visited the copy room at the end of the hall to photocopy that week-old memo for the fourth time that day, in hopes of catching a glimpse of their crush at his desk on the way? And then, having finally worked up the courage to speak to that cute guy over the wall of his cubicle, found herself rambling incoherently about toner and paper jams. Why do we fabricate excuses to be near a crush only to choke when the time comes to actually speak to him? Because a) we need our fix and b) when we get that fix, our brains are so bombarded by crush dopamine that even the most basic motor functions become challenging.

April Rose

Every guy that was older than me I had a crush on: my teacher, my brother's friends, my friends' dads—major daddy complex crusher.

Most of the time, crushes are harmless fun. The crushes come and go and, despite the odd embarrassing moment or lapse in judgment, life goes on. Just like the time we did a couple of bong hits with our friends in college, got all giggly and drove to Taco Bell in our pajamas. But then there are the kinds of crushes that are so hardcore, we lose ourselves down the rabbit hole. We find ourselves obsessively checking his status for updates at two o'clock in the morning, or dragging our friends across town because Foursquare says he just checked in to some lame-ass sports bar, or joining his fantasy football league under a fake name so we can feel "closer" to him. If you are exhibiting these kinds of behaviors, and especially if you are a repeat offender, you are in danger of becoming a junky crush-stalker.

In her insightful analysis on this parallel between intoxication and infatuation, aptly titled "Your Love Is My Drug," Ke$ha Rose Sebert—who, according to her lyrics, has done extensive research on both intoxicants and hooking up with guys (often using herself as a case study)—writes of the potential pitfalls of the

Alice Wetterlund

The crush to obsession line lies somewhere in the middle of that scarf you're knitting for him.

CRUSH

OBSESSION

hardcore crush, "My steeze is gonna be affected if I keep it up like a lovesick crackhead." Wise words. If you have reached the point where you have the judgment and self-control of a tweaker in a meth lab, it's time to pull back and take stock of yourself. The problem with this kind of crush is that it has the potential to become more about the rush than actually attaining the guy. You are so busy chasing the high you get from the crush, you fail to see that the guy you've fixated on isn't a complex and tortured artist, he's just a loser with a neck tattoo, 12-gauge plugs in his earlobes, and a part-time job at Trader Joe's.

CRUSH RED FLAGS

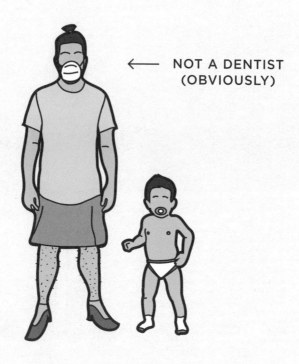

← NOT A DENTIST
(OBVIOUSLY)

Jessimae Peluso

If you're gonna tell a dude you have a crush on him, you need to prepare yourself for the risk of him telling you some information you don't want to hear: he's got kids, he's really got a vagina, he's got halitosis, no insurance, he's really not a dentist. Are you prepared for that shit?

So how do you know when a harmless crush has become a fatal attraction? Ask yourself:

- ⭕ Are you having more conversations with him in your head than you are in real life?
- ⭕ Are you using social media to chart his every move?
- ⭕ Have you pieced together your own backstory of his childhood from photos tagged on his Facebook page?
- ⭕ Do you habitually check his horoscope to see if your sun will align with his moon?
- ⭕ Have you graduated from mentally hyphenating your last name and his, to naming your three unborn children and imaginary pet labradoodle?

If you answered yes to more than one of these questions, your crush has become a compulsion. If you answered yes to all five, you have likely hit rock bottom.

Carly Aquilino

I was in the neighborhood, so I figured I'd just stop into this barber shop and just hang out and wait for you—and smell you, and hug you, and embrace you.

UNACCEPTABLE METHODS OF CRUSH RESEARCH

NSA data harvest
Amateur telepathy
Military grade binoculars
Crystal anything
Reconnaissance drone

Felony stalking
CSI his locker
Summoning spirits
FBI wiretap
An advance bionic ear
Asking him yourself

Fortunately for all of us, Girl Code is here to help. We're all familiar with AA's Twelve-Step program for alcoholics and drug addicts, Girl Code has it's own simplified Four-Step program for recovery from a crush addiction (we've boiled it down to four steps because, let's be honest, this just isn't that complicated). Think of Girl Code as your higher power and the following steps as a set of guiding principles for getting your crush behavior back on track:

1 Admit that we are powerless over our crush addiction—that our judgment and emotional reactions had become self-defeating and inappropriate when we crossed the line from harmless infatuation to creepy stalker obsession.

2 Come to believe and trust in the power and wisdom of Girl Code, like a big sister who will smack us on the back of the head when we attempt to "run out" for milk at the bodega on our crush's corner, even though it's twenty blocks from where we live.

3 Make a searching and fearless moral inventory of ourselves and recognize that it is wrong to Facebook creep on a crush's friends and family, or to sleep in the hoodie we stole off the back of his chair while he was at lunch.

4 Having had a spiritual awakening as the result of these steps, we vow to stop crushing on unattainable guys and thereby break the cycle of crush addiction, to carry this message to other crush addicts, and to practice the principles of Girl Code in all our affairs of the heart.

The intent here is not to frighten you into a "Just Say No!" stance on crushes. Like a glass of red wine with dinner at the end of the day, a little recreational crushing is good for the heart. The key is moderation and self-control. It's okay to have fantasies about that hot fireman who shops for his station house at your local grocery store. Not okay to start a fire in your kitchen because that fantasy involves him falling in love with you after he carries you in his arms from the smoking ruins of your apartment building.

GirlCode:

DON'T GET CRUSHED BY YOUR OWN OBSESSION.

Flirting

Sachi Ezura

**Flirting allows you to keep your dignity
intact if it turns out he's just not that into you.**

Carly Aquilino

Tricks for being a good flirt: lean in towards him, laugh at everything he says even though it's not funny, and maybe whisper something in his ear very playful like, "How big is your dick?"

gh. Flirting. I can't even make the girls in my office like me, let alone cute stranger boys in bars. So why do we flirt? What's the point? If a guy is into you, can't you just be like "You. Me. Sex. Now." Sure, that would be easier. But unfortunately we don't always know whether a guy is into us. And if you're not a hundred percent sure how a guy feels about you, you need a way to subtly let him know that you are interested. Flirting allows you to keep your dignity intact if it turns out he's just not that into you.

But HOW do you do that?? For a long time, I had no idea what I was doing. When I was in high school, boys seemed like this alien species and all I wanted to do was make contact. But instead of just talking to them like they were normal people, I would go cuckoo bananas any time a guy tried to talk to me. I didn't mean to be a spaz. I'd think of witty, classy things to say that would communicate my attraction coherently, but somehow between my brain and my mouth, they'd get all jumbled up and come out sounding like I was an autistic four-year-old. I read a shit ton of lady magazines and despite their offering somewhat good advice, I managed to misinterpret everything they told me to do.

RELATIONSHIP
~~LOVE~~ SHACK

FLIRTING

FUN HOUSE

FLIRTING

Jessimae Peluso

Good flirting can be the foundation to a great relationship. Or it can just be the foundation to fun.

What *Cosmo* Said:	What I Did:
Have confidence.	Act like you are too cool for school. Fill your life with so many activities that you never have time for anybody but yourself.
Be yourself.	Don't feel embarrassed of anything you do. If you need alcohol for that, drink a lot of it. Talk to strangers. Do cartwheels in public. Touch people you don't know. Regret nothing.
Have a sense of humor.	Make fun of boys. Find reasons to touch them, even if it's hitting. Laugh at their stupid jokes, preferably in a cackle-y ungirly way. Point out to them when they are wrong and do not back down.
Cast a wide net.	Have no standards. Experiment with bisexuality. Like anyone that likes you.
Find ways to meet new people.	Do things you don't really like. Go to football games or comic book conventions, despite your complete lack of interest.
Be complicated and mysterious.	If a guy is nice to you, cry. If he is mean to you, cry—but then like him more.
When all else fails, love yourself.	Never go outside. Clearly, human beings are too much to deal with. It's not worth it.

Okay, so clearly I was not an expert in the art of flirtation. But despite my chaotic and unhealthy style of seduction, I occasionally found boys who had some inconceivable interest me, and eventually, against all odds, I got a real boyfriend. The good thing about having a real boyfriend —not one of those guys you just call your boyfriend in your head—is that you can ask him exactly what worked and what didn't. "Why did you like me? When did you first think I was cute? Was there ever a point where you wanted to kiss me but didn't have the balls?" These are questions that are appropriate to ask a boyfriend, but not a second date.

Nicole Byer

We're flirting to get a drink.
We're flirting to get a date.
We're flirting to get screwed.
We're flirting for a new wig.

  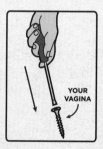 

A few weeks after my first serious boyfriend and I had that define-the-relationship convo, I made some joke about how I was a master flirt. And he was like, "Uh, yeah, okay…," which actually meant, "Ha ha ha—you think you're good at flirting? You are a spazzy mess with sauce on your shirt, but lucky for you I find that charming." Obviously this prompted a long and self-conscious conversation about how, if I wasn't crushing it flirt-wise, did I get the guy (aka him) in the end? And here's what Serious Boyfriend #1 said: "You try so hard to be cool and aloof that I honestly thought you hated me for the first two weeks." Ladies, this is the moment where I learned that all my attempts at flirting were being completely misread. It turns out there's a fine line between playing hard-to-get and acting like a cold hard bitch.

Unfortunately, the opposite approach—complete honesty and approachability—isn't foolproof either. But it's worth trying at least once in your life. Go up to a guy in a bar, tell him he's cute and see what happens. The worst that can happen is he's like "No, thank you. I prefer beautiful thin girls." Yes, it sucks to hear, but you walk out of the bar still alive and realize that no matter what life throws at you, you will survive. Now that I've tried being both completely available and totally aloof, it's a lot easier to find the happy medium between the two.

Melanie Iglesias

We give hints. We'll twirl our hair around or touch his shoulder. We'll find any reason to touch a guy that we like. We can't help it.

NEW ABBREVIATIONS FOR TEXT FLIRTING

QT(_|_) – Cute butt
MLTMF – Make love to my face
LHC – Let's have children
CITOY – Can I twerk on you?
IAW – I'm already wet
YMG – You're my Gosling

LBDP –
Let's be domestic partners
ABG – Awkward boob graze
TOYW – Thinking of your wang
IMYB – I'll make you breakfast
;-O – Winky orgasm face

Jessimae Peluso

When a dude flirts with you, sometimes you don't realize it because you're too busy being self-conscious. You're like, "How could he really like me?" He likes you. If he's touching you, he likes you—unless you're bleeding and he's trying to help you.

LIKES YOU   SAVING YOUR LIFE

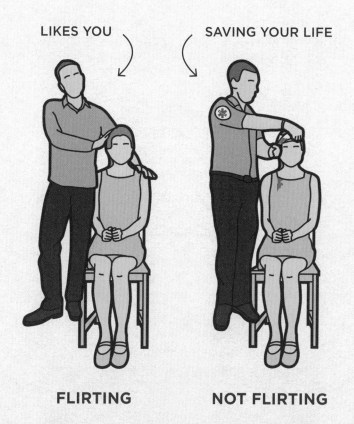

FLIRTING   **NOT FLIRTING**

Flirting is not some magical formula that allows you to transform the hot guy in your co-ed softball league into your personal sex slave. It's about being the coolest, most approachable version of yourself you can be. The key to flirting is simply putting yourself out there. Talking to strangers is like any other skill—it takes practice to get good at it, just like riding a bicycle, playing piano or giving blow jobs. If you're on the shyer side, find a super-

Nicole Byer

I am not a good flirt. I'm just very heavy handed. If I think my waiter's cute, I will put my number on the check and I'll be like, "Call this, heh heh heh."

GUEST CHECK

12 inch Sausage 6 00
Bowl of Peaches 4 00

total 10 00

♥ 850·167·2224

NICOLE'S FLIRTING TECHNIQUE

outgoing friend you can bring with you as a wing-woman. Then just make it a rule to talk to anyone who seems moderately approachable. If unattractive guys talk to you, use them as practice for the cuties that will follow once you get great. (Also true of blow jobs.) Plus, even if the guy you're talking to isn't good-looking, you never know who he might know. Maybe he's Ryan Reynolds's tax attorney or Channing Tatum's dentist. Isn't it worth it to talk to the guy who gets to legally put his hands in Channing Tatum's mouth? (Isn't it worth it to blow him?)

Flirting can be really stressful because you are in a state of not knowing. You want more than anything to know that someone likes you and to communicate that you like them, too. It's easy to forget that the not knowing part is supposed to be fun. You get to wink and smile and touch him and be cute. You get to freak out with your girl friends about what every text message means. You only get to do those things for so long. Then suddenly, in one brilliant lovely moment, everything comes together and you realize you really do like each other. That moment is only great because of all the not knowing that led up to it. Enjoy the flirtation, the chase, the process of sending out signals and getting them back, because one day, when you finally get the guy, when he's falling asleep in your arms watching Netflix and covered in Cheetos dust, you'll find it hard to believe that you ever tried so hard to impress him.

GirlCode:
—

PRACTICE MAKES TOLERABLE.

Friend Zone

Laura Murphy

I am pretty sure I'm the only girl in history
to have uttered the phrase, "I wish I could find
a guy who just wants me for my body."

Carly Aquilino

We put guys in the Friend Zone that are really sweet to us and say and do nice things for us. But we're like, "Aw, you're my best friend. I would never date you."

 am pretty sure the term "Friend Zone" was invented by a guy (who may or may not have worked at a water park at some point). First of all, it rhymes with End Zone. Second, it is a deceptively clean, clear, and simple name for a type of relationship that can be very messy, murky, and confusing. Or at least for women it is. Left to our own devices, we would have named it "That Zone Where You Wait for a Guy to Change His Mind About You, Sometimes Successfully Sometimes Not, and Where You Can Keep Guys You Will Never Sleep with in Case You Need Help Moving or Installing An Air Conditioner." Not quite as catchy, though. So, thanks Guy Who Coined Friend Zone. We owe you one.

For the most part, we all know what it means to Friend-Zone a guy. We've all done it, for various reasons, and barring the occasional backlash, it usually works out for us in the end. But *being* Friend-Zoned . . . that is where the real complications and questions arise. How do you avoid it? With patience, can the Friend Zone be a layover on the way to Relationship Town? What happens if you have been Friend-Zoned so many times and have so many guy friends that it feels like nobody will ever want to date you? I don't know shit about the first two questions. But I can definitely answer that last one.

WISHFUL THINKING

Shalyah Evans

I got super Friend-Zoned by a guy when I was nineteen. I still haven't quite given up. I'm still like, "No, no, no, this could still turn around any minute now."

Considering I looked like a slightly effeminate Charlie Sheen until I was twenty, I did alright in high school. I had a boyfriend. In fact, he was older—like college old. To be honest, this situation only came about because none of the boys at my high school could get past my short hair, flat chest, and the fact that my dad was a teacher there. But when you are a boyish sixteen-year-old, it's easier not to dwell on those details and to just revel in the fact that any guy is dating you at all. Not to mention, said guy had a car and cool-older-guy friends who threw cool-older-guy parties.

Suddenly, my weekends were filled with beer pong parties in basements and jokes and stories shared over kegs. At first, I would just observe, laugh, and formulate in my head how I would brag about this to my classmates on Monday. But then something happened that changed the way I interacted with the male species forever. One night, feeling emboldened by several Solo cups of watery beer, I made a joke. The guys were talking about a girl who had a fake rack and I said, "If you rub one of her boobs against your hair really fast, you can stick it to the wall." Slightly conceptual for a first joke, but it just tumbled out of my mouth before I realized what I was saying. Suddenly, it got quiet. Everyone turned and looked at me, as if they had just noticed I was there. Then, after the longest second in history, they all burst out laughing. This was the greatest moment of my high school life. I was hooked.

Eventually, the boyfriend moved on to a girl his own age, but I continued to hang out with all his friends. They invited me to everything: movies, concerts, poker nights. I mean, these guys seemingly couldn't get enough of me. It was only a matter of time before I would be dating another one of them, right? This is the stuff high school movies are made of. Wanting to show off and prove to the more attractive, popular girls at school that boys liked me, too (hot older

 Nicole Byer

~~~

I live in the Friend Zone. Guys are always like, "Nicole, you're so funny. You're a good friend." I don't want to be your friend. I want to suck your cock.

Tanisha Long

If you want to get out of the Friend Zone you just gotta be brave and make a move. But know that you might get kicked out of the Friend Zone and not put into the Girlfriend Zone. You might just get kicked out of all the Zones.

YOU ARE HERE

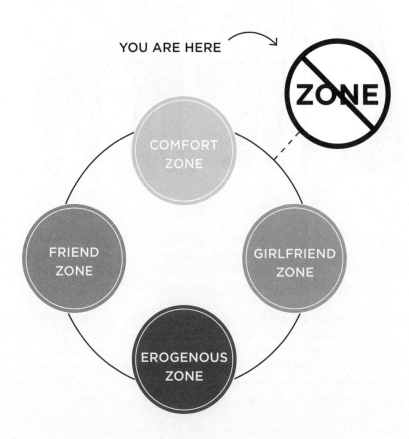

GUYS WHO BELONG IN THE FRIEND ZONE

boys at that), I started inviting my classmates to all the parties. Within a week, my cool-older-guy friends were hooking up with every girl I introduced them to. That's when I realized it was just my personality they couldn't get enough of. They didn't want to date me. I had been group Friend-Zoned.

This realization was ego crushing. But, being sixteen, I tried to see the positive side. At least I was still in the inner circle. The guys still confided in me when they weren't into the girls, and I was there when they made fun of some of them behind their backs. I pushed past the insecurity about not being wanted, because at least I was still on the inside. But I was the only girl who didn't have a real date for the prom and I spent the rest of high school single.

By the time I went off to college, the pattern was already ingrained. When I met a guy, my first instinct was to make him laugh. My second was to assume

he wasn't physically attracted to me. So I acted accordingly. I would spend months hanging out with guys I was really into, pretending I wasn't attracted to them and they would end up dating other girls who made the first move. I endlessly complained to my girl friends about my predicament. I'm pretty sure I'm

Alesha Reneé

Have more confidence in yourself. Men love confidence. Just walk up to him and, in the back of your mind, know that it is in his best interest to be into all of this.

the only girl in history to have uttered the phrase, "I wish I could find a guy who just wants me for my body."

I realize now, the kind of insecurity I was struggling with is the kind that feeds on itself. If you go into a situation expecting a negative outcome, you will 100% create a scenario where that is the only possible outcome. And every time that pattern repeats, you feed the insecurity a little more. Essentially, I was preemptively Friend-Zoning myself with guys—acting like a friend, then wondering why they only saw me in that light. What a dummy.

During my junior year, I was home from college for the holidays and heard from one of the guys from that old crew that I hung out with in high school. Time and separation afforded me the confidence to actually ask him why none of them had ever made a move on me. Was I not hot enough? What he said blew my mind. It had nothing to do with looks. None of them wanted to hook up with me because if they did and fucked it up, as they tended to do with girls, I wouldn't be around anymore. And they liked having me around. Plus, they respected me. He added that they had all agreed that I was super cute, but that I wasn't the type of girl you should just fool around with. I was the type you should lock down and be with for real. Which was a nice touch.

SIGNS YOU'RE LEAVING THE FRIEND ZONE AND ENTERING THE MOTHER ZONE

You bring him soup every time he's sick	You do his laundry (but you don't live together)
You take him shopping for clothes (that he'll use to get laid by other girls)	He keeps trying to set you up with his divorced dad
He asks you to "come take a look at this weird rash for me"	You pick out his gifts for his mom, even though you've never met her
You lick your finger and use it to wipe something off of his face	You are taking care of him and not getting shit in return
You cut his food for him	He tells you that you remind him of his mom

Jessimae Peluso

A flick of the hair. Put some perfume on.
A little bit of tit cleavage. A little bit. Quarter
of an inch. That's enough. He can imagine the
other six inches.

JUST A LITTLE BIT

Now, I am fully aware that he might have just said all of that to make me feel better. I look back at pictures of me then and "bang-able" isn't exactly the word that comes to mind. But that conversation caused a shift in my perspective and helped me break out of the whole Friend Zone pattern I had been stuck in. I was no longer going to fear rejection before it even happened because I could be missing out on a real opportunity. I headed back to college with a mission of putting myself out there. And promptly got rejected by the first three dudes I tried to make out with. But I stayed friends with one of them and you know what? My ego survived it. Plus, the fourth guy I made a move on became my boyfriend for four years.

What I am trying to say is: the Friend Zone might have been named by a guy, but us girls are really good at putting ourselves in it before they even get a chance to. I am not advising you to throw yourself at every older guy you think is hot, that's not a good idea at all (it's also how political scandals start). But the Girl Codey approach is that if you're really feeling a guy, and there is a friendship forming, it can't hurt to make a move.

Rejection does sting, but bruises to your ego heal quickly and guys are fairly resilient when it comes to rejecting you. (Note: they are not as resilient when you reject *them*.) You'd be surprised how quickly the awkwardness disappears and you can both be cool again. (If the awkwardness doesn't disappear, then eff them, you don't need those kinds of friends anyway.) But if they make an honest effort to build a platonic relationship afterward, give it a try. Being someone's favorite person (other than your parents') just because of who you are is pretty awesome. And getting used to that feeling doesn't hurt when you meet someone who feels that way *and* wants to have sex with you. Plus, hilarious guy friends, who will always have your back, even when it comes to another guy, are what high school movies *should* be made about.

GirlCode:

MAKE A MOVE OR MAKE IT YOUR HOME.

First Dates

Brooke Van Poppelen

You shouldn't be meeting up with him and a group of friends at a house party. It should just be the two of you. Otherwise, newsflash: you're not on a date.

Alice Wetterlund

Usually, you go on a "thing" and then at the very end you realize it's a date 'cause you sleep with the guy.

I f I had to name three things that really terrify me (death excluded), they would have to be skydiving, scuba diving, and first dates. Yes, first dates are right up there with falling out of a plane only to discover midair that you have a faulty parachute, or getting lost in a coral reef one mile below the surface of the ocean with only fifteen minutes of oxygen left in your tank. They're all exciting things that have the potential to end horribly.

First, let me clarify that "hanging out" is not a first date. What in the eff is up with guys who ask you if you want to "hang sometime"? It's noncommittal and childish, yet we fall for it all the time. We get stuck in the Hang Out Zone, which is akin to the Friend Zone, and no one wants to be there! Dating is really confusing and "hanging out" is a super safe, low-stakes option. It's like pre-gaming the date. But if the dude is seriously interested and wants to pursue you, he should man up and officially ask you out. Also, just in case you weren't sure, you shouldn't be meeting up with him and a group of friends at a house party. It should be just the two of you, otherwise, newsflash: you're not on a date.

Glad we got that out of the way. So, once you've found a guy who has the balls and manners to actually ask you out on a date, *he* should be the one to come up with a plan. There's a chance he'll choose a Guy Fieri restaurant or a Michael Bay movie, but even if you hate every living moment of the stuff he chooses to do, at least you'll know pretty quickly what you're getting into with him. In so many ways first dates are like an audition in which you are both trying out for the role of "future something." It could be "future significant other" if it goes well, or "future awkward encounter at the supermarket while buying kitty

MAKE EYE CONTACT

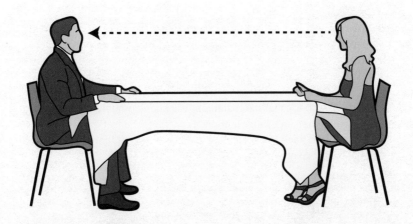

Tanisha Long

A great thing to do is make a lot of eye contact with the guy. It's also good to test him to see if he's okay with eye contact because some guys get freaked out by that.

litter and tampons" if it does not.

Am I painting a negative picture? I'm not trying to. First dates should be really fun and flirty if you're doing it right. Girl Code says you should go on lots of first dates—it's part of the romance and relationship game. They just can't all be winners, ya know? It's exciting and nerve-wracking when casual flirting turns into something formal—otherwise known as an ACTUAL PLAN.

So congratulations, you're going on a date! Before you get too excited there is a Girl Code plan of attack that must be followed so that you come out on top. Heh, heh—see what I did there?

Food (and Booze) For Thought

Food dates can be a little tough sometimes because you're already nervous and now you have to eat in front of someone. Aside from worrying about my manners, I've got some allergies and dietary restrictions so ordering can make me look really picky and un-fun. To save face I check out the menu online in advance and make a mental note of what I can eat. I've even called ahead to double check that the restaurant will accommodate my order if I'm going to a place that isn't super friendly to my diet. The last thing you want on a first date is to have to explain to a prickly waiter, "If there's dairy in my entrée, my ass will explode!"

Definitely make sure you eat enough because where there is food, there is sure to be booze and you don't want to be drinking with one leaf of lettuce in your stomach. I generally don't take life advice from *Millionaire Matchmaker* Patty Stanger, but she enforces a two-drink maximum on dates and it's brilliant. When I get nervous, to calm the anxiety I have a tendency to have one too many. I've done this on dates before and one time I quickly went from charming and witty Brooke to foul-mouthed, slurring, kicked-over-a-trash can Brooke. Know your limits. And if your drink of choice is straight vodka, limit yourself to one.

Conversation Killa

The art of conversation takes some time to master so be gentle with yourself, little grasshopper. There will be some lulls and awkward moments. Passionate discussions about politics and religion are cool if you are both on the same side of the fence, but generally this is dangerous territory. Maybe start with something more pop-culture friendly, like discussing your feelings about Jamie Dornan replacing Charlie Hunnam as Christian Grey in the *Fifty Shades of Grey* movie. Hmmm. On second thought, maybe keep the hotties out of the convo and talk about how insanely awesome and brutal *The Walking Dead* is and where you picture Rick Grimes leading the gang next. If you live in a cave and don't have Internet or TV, your best bet is to ask him what he's into and be an attentive listener. Guys love to talk as much as girls do.

Alice Wetterlund

Don't talk about how many kids you want to have, but you should say how many kids you *do* have.

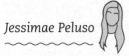

Jessimae Peluso

No politics. Don't talk about jail. Don't talk about your vegan activism, he doesn't want to hear about it.

UNACCEPTABLE FIRST DATES TOPICS

The Hook Up

Hooking up on a first date is always a hot topic among girls. Girl Code would never tell you whether or not you should sleep with a guy on the first date. It's entirely situational, so you just have to feel it out. Heh—see what I did again there? With my current boyfriend I decided to hold out and build up our relationship before jumping right into bed with him. I won't tell you how long I waited because, honestly, it's not that impressive. But still, even if you hold out 'til a third date that's exercising some level of control and if you really like a guy it can be worth the wait.

On the other hand, I've had plenty of dates that I went into hopeful for a relationship and then realized that, although he wasn't really boyfriend mate-rial, he was perfect sex material. (For more on this see our chapter on Friends with Benefits.) You're single, you're horny—so is he, hopefully—and at least he isn't a perfect stranger. You've talked a few times, spent an evening together, and you know his name, phone number, and address. Girl, you've just found yourself the perfect "maintenance sex" partner, so get it!

SIGNS IT'S NOT REALLY A DATE

Everybody's puking

The manager just asked
you all to leave

A bunch of people just
fell through the ice

The "menu" you're holding is
a public urination ticket

The line's not bad,
for the post office

Its some cool new place called
*Tommy's Mom's House
She's Out of Town*

You had to hop a fence

You're at a bus stop

There's ample parking
(it's a parking lot)

The sparkle in his eye
is oncoming traffic

It Ain't Over Til It's Over

So you had a good first date. Congrats! It's the end of the night, now what? Here are the several ways it can go down and how you should handle each scenario:

Esther Ku
〜〜〜〜

What I do is I just make sure I don't wax
or shave down there. Just keep it a big mess,
so you're not even tempted to do it.

1 If you received a kiss goodnight, there's a pretty good chance you are advancing to round two of the dating game. Ding ding ding ding ding!!! In this instance, sending a follow up text the same night or the next morning is totally fine.

2 If there was no kiss, but the guy says he'd like to see you again, okay. That's something. But here's the thing, LET HIM FOLLOW UP. Resist the urge to text, DM, Facebook, or call. If he wants to ask you out again, he will. He didn't forget.

3 If he was a complete jerk and the date was a disaster, walk away. You don't even have to wait until the end of the date. Leave mid-dinner. Eff that guy. No explanation, follow up, or phone call is necessary.

Carly Aquilino
~~~~~~~~~~~~~~~~

If you wait three days for him to call and he doesn't call you: he's married. He has a wife and kids. That's just what you need to tell yourself.

Having a code to live by when you're on a first date will help you make it to that second date. If you apply these tips and strategies to the uncertain chaos that is dating, you're going to minimize the terror of it all and end up feeling excited and in control, which are both attractive qualities. And remember, first dates should be a fun experience for us girls and even if they're not, hey free food! You're breaking Girl Code if you turn your back on some free food, so get out there and go on a date!

GirlCode:
_____
LUCKILY THERE'S ONLY ONE.

Foreplay

Laura Murphy

**You need to set the precedent
early on that there will be no
penetration without proper stimulation.**

Esther Ku

Foreplay is the part of sex that girls like.

alk outside right now, go to the nearest establishment dealing in magazines, skate past the gossip mag section and put the brakes on before you hit the porn rack. Count how many covers have teasers for articles about the best ways to get him ready before he gets it in. There's a sea of mastheads flanked by cover lines like: "Have Hotter Sex Tonight," "What To Do With A Naked man (That You Haven't Thought of Yet)," and "Heat Up The Action Before the Action." Admittedly, I haven't read all of the articles. But if they are anything like the similarly repetitive promises of "Five Thigh Busting Exercises That Will Blow Your Mind," it's the same old tips repackaged to sound new.

We all know that traditionally a foreplay session includes one or more of the following: neck licking, ear blowing, finger blasting, dry humping, nipple kissing, dirty talking, motorboating, hand jobs, over-the-pants hand jobs, no-look hand jobs, other kinds of lesser known hand jobs, and oral sex. In theory, a combination of several of these things is implemented in a manner that builds in intensity, thereby successfully getting all parties lubed up to eventually close the deal (hopefully it is not a combination of all of them because that is a lot of hand jobs). But what about the lesser discussed, nonphysical, pre-foreplay foreplay? What about the *beforeplay*?

DIFFERENT TYPES OF FOREPLAY

MAKING OUT

HEAVY PETTING

FRENCH TOUCHING

So much of how we operate, how we perceive ourselves, and how we feel comes from mental stimuli. I challenge you to find one girl that isn't super turned on by the thought of the perfect guy showering her with attention, listening to her stories, telling her she is amazing, gazing into her eyes, really being present, complimenting her style/body/personality and *then* wanting to bang the shit out of her. The real challenge isn't just finding someone who knows how to "rev" your "engine" physically. You're not a car. The real challenge is finding someone who can get you all hot and bothered while your clothes are still on. And then keep turning you on while he takes them off.

Your average ladies magazine isn't going to tell you this but whether it is a fling, a one-night stand, or the beginning stages of a relationship, talking is a huge part of what turns us on. If you are really attracted to a guy, he can tell you a story about the time he stole a loaf of bread when he was thirteen and your underwear will get all squishy. Or he will stare wide-eyed and enraptured as you recount the drama surrounding the play you wrote and performed in fifth grade, barely able to keep his hands off of you until the end. All in all, these are the glory days. Enjoy them because they will not last forever.

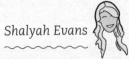 *Shalyah Evans*

Roleplaying can be a cool part of foreplay as long as you are on the same page.

In the beginning of a relationship, the beforeplay comes naturally . . . because there is so much talking. But, as time goes on, you've heard all the stories, he stops sharing new ones, you both get a little lazy in the effort department and when the compliments dry up, so do your lady parts. Next thing you know, he just wants to play Madden, pause it to hump, then go back to playing until he falls asleep. Is there a way to avoid this lackluster phase that will likely carry on until the eventual slow death of your shared sex life? Probably not. But there are a couple preventative steps that can be taken early on to stave it off for a while.

Make out for just a little too long with your clothes on.
This especially applies if it is a first-time hook up. Kissing is super intimate and it is also a great way to test a guy's patience. Consider making out to be the saliva-coated segue between beforeplay and foreplay. It's also like a speed bump to slow down the action and give you a chance to change your mind. If the dude is rushing the make out, he's most likely gonna Jeff Gordon it through the rest of the pre-penetration acts—if he does them at all.

Take my word for it, there are only two reasons a guy would try to finger bang you three seconds into kissing, while your jeans are still on: because he is so hot for you he can't contain himself (in which case telling him to slow down will make him even hotter) or because sex is what he came there for and he doesn't feel like wasting any more time (in which case telling him to slow down will probably annoy him and you should kick him out).

Nicole Byer

Foreplay is all about your tongue and your hands—and maybe your feet if you're a freak.

Don't ever skip the physical foreplay.
As I said, when you are in that tingly butterflies part of a new relationship, the mentally engaging beforeplay sometimes does the job on its own. He's like "you're gorgeous" and you're like "yup, I'm ready, put it in." Bad idea. Even if you don't need it, make him do the physical work up front. You need to set the precedent early on that there will be no penetration without proper stimulation (this is up for grabs as a campaign slogan if anyone wants it).

Even if your brain is doing the heavy lifting on the lubing in the beginning, when that stops happening, you need something to fall back on—like his mouth or his fingers. For the greater good of girls everywhere, don't let him slip by (literally) without putting in the work. If he isn't automatically going down on you or making sure you get off before diving in, it's because girls before you have failed you and if you don't insist then the next girl will have an even harder time

TAKE A NATURE WALK

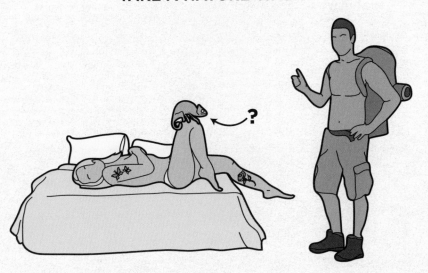

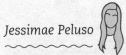

Jessimae Peluso

If a guy doesn't want to explore your body, he's a loser. Have fun. Take a nature walk. There's some butterflies over there. Look at the beautiful geraniums. Where'd the lizard come from? I don't know, pet it. Pet it for forty-five minutes.

demanding it. If we all think of it as group training and insist every time, it will make all of our lives easier in the long run.

Oh, and when you insist, do it in a sexy way. You can say you want him to "see" how hot you are and hope he gets the hint. I have definitely used the "I want you to feel how hot you make me" trick and just put his fingers where I wanted them. Saying something to the effect of "I want to make this last as long as possible" is also a good way to slow down the process and hint at wanting more foreplay. Whatever you do, make it happen and avoid ordering him around. Unless of course you are both into that, then order away.

One final note on this: if you go out with a guy multiple times or end up in a relationship, don't overuse this trick. It is most effective when used sparingly. If you aren't creative enough to find different ways to say it, only do it once in a while or they might catch on. Once they realize we are doing this as a strategy, it'll be ruined for all of us.
If you are a guy reading this, please forget what you just read . . . Oh, look over there! Sports things. Boobies.

Tell him you want more talking.
And clarify that you mean before sex. Because if he misunderstands and thinks you want him to talk more during sex, it can get real awkward real fast. Girl Code is about making sure you get yours, and it's okay for part of 'yours' to be feeling connected before you do it. Guys think of foreplay as the seven-to-nine minutes right before getting it in. You need to explain that they can lay the groundwork to getting laid all day long, without even really trying that hard. Attention and flattery go a long way. In fact, if you explain that taking twenty seconds to complement you and pretending to listen when you talk, will guarantee more sex and save them one-to-two minutes of physical foreplay, they will probably thank you.

If he's given it his all, it doesn't hurt for you to do it too.
If you haven't figured it out yet, the pre-sex blowie is kind of a win/win. He gets a bj, so he is happy, and since it is just a warm up to sex, you don't have to spend too much time on it. Somehow this cuts down on the requests for non-foreplay related bjs. I'm not sure why this works, but trust me, it does.

WORST NAMES FOR FOREPLAY MOVES

Schenectady Snow Pants	Guadalajara Hard Hat
Backhanded Salamander	Hamburg Handlebars
Bolivian Leotard	Tofu Tikka Masala
Moroccan Chapstick	Whitewashin' Tom Sawyer
The Slow Ferry to Martha's Vineyard	Canadian Brisket
Dachshund in a Duane Reade	The Airport Shuttle
	Low Country Spinach Dip

There is plenty of Code to foreplay. Most of it boils down to you enjoying sex as much as he does and not being afraid to ask for whatever you need to do that. So think outside the box, or more specifically, outside just him touching your box (but make sure he does that too). True intimacy comes from more than just groping, rubbing, licking and touching. Let him warm up your ego before he warms everything else up. Not only will the sex be better, but your relationship might just last longer . . . or at least take longer to get boring, which is a small victory in the grand scheme of things.

Hell, even if you don't end up with the guy in the long run, you'll be doing a huge favor for all the girls he will hook up with in the future. Frankly, you're a hero. Girl Code.

GirlCode:

THE SQUEAKY WHEEL GETS THE GREASE.

Morning
After

Sachi Ezura

Best case scenario, you wake up in your own bed clutching a bag of half-eaten Doritos and realize that the worst thing you did last night was break your juice cleanse.

Tanisha Long

The morning after is when everything stops being sexy, and starts being real stinky and, like, vomity.

ike the opening scene of *Lost*, my eyes pop open and I attempt to gauge my surroundings. My hair is matted into a tangle of curls. My contacts are still in, although looking through them is like wearing cotton balls as glasses. One of my earrings is missing. My mouth is dry and tastes vaguely of tequila and regret.

I am wearing a Georgetown T-shirt (not mine) and a pair of pantyhose (mine). That's a good sign. The fact that they are still on after last night's debauchery means I did not have sex. If I had had sex, I certainly would not have drunkenly decided to put them back on. Even sober, putting on pantyhose is a chore reminiscent of stuffing sausage into its casing. Like a slutty Sherlock Holmes, I piece together that I may have rounded third base, but luckily I never went home. *Ha, home,* I think. If I were a smarter girl, I would have gone home two hours before last call.

EXPENSE IT

Jessimae Peluso

If you can remember what happened last night, and it wasn't horrific, sure go for round two. But if you wake up and realize you took home the taxi cab driver? Get your receipt and get out. You can at least expense it.

Jessimae Peluso

In the morning you're like, "I didn't really need to do Jagermeister shots. I normally don't, but this guy said he was a tennis player from Australia." No, he's a fence installer with malaria.

WITH JÄGER SHOTS

WITHOUT JÄGER SHOTS

I vaguely remember the cab ride back here (a sloppy make-out session, which our driver had to endure) and realize that I am in Brooklyn. I find my phone wedged between his bed and the wall and discover that it's dead. Great. Now I get to sit quietly on the subway and think about what I've done. No podcasts or Candy Crush Saga to distract me from whatever grossness happened last night.

YOU'RE NOT GETTING BREAKFAST IN BED

Welcome to the Morning After. Best case scenario, you wake up in your own bed clutching a half-eaten bag of Doritos and realize that the worst thing you did last night was break your juice cleanse. Yeah, Best Case Scenario left when your best friend ditched you last night to make out with the bartender. More likely, the Morning After occurs after you've made a number of mistakes, including but not limited to 1) going to a stranger's house and 2) hooking up with said stranger. Didn't your mom ever tell you not to talk to strangers? You may have a hangover and cottonmouth, but you should be glad you weren't murdered. STRANGER DANGER. STRANGER DANGER.

When I was thirteen, I fantasized that if you stayed over at a guy's apartment, you'd wake up swathed in 1,000-thread count sheets, sunlight streaming through the window. "Good morning, sleepyhead," he'd say as he carried in homemade pancakes on a tray. "You were wonderful last night, darling. Perfectly classy with the slightest hint of freak in the sheets. You definitely didn't throw up on my penis." "Thank you," you'd say. "It was certainly a pleasure, but I'd best be on my way." He would beg you not to go, promising a day of bird-watching and strawberry-picking. But you have a very busy career as a Broadway actress/food critic/vampire slayer, and so you'd leave him crying into his delicious chocolate-chip pancakes. Well, most of them. Obvs, you'd take one for the road.

Yeah, somehow that's not how my life turned out.

I have never ever had someone make me breakfast in bed. The nicest thing anyone's ever done for me after a one night stand is buy me Dunkin Donuts on my way to the train station. And even then he was pretty specific that I could only get a donut, not an egg sandwich. Maybe that's more indicative of the kind of broke scrubs I used to hook up with. Maybe there are girls out there who've had lovely Morning After situations, where they ended up spending the whole weekend together and realized they were soul mates. To those girls, I say kudos, you clearly have better drunk taste than I do. This chapter is not for you, you stupid lucky girl.

Let's say you're not that girl, that you're more like me and you've woken up somewhere unfamiliar with someone unfamiliar. The trick now is to get out quickly and gracefully. I know, grace does not come easily when you can't find your panties.

Alesha Reneé
~~~~~~~

Do not stay and linger on throughout the day.
"So, what are we doing today?"
We just did what we were doing today.

A couple of helpful hints to make the most of your Morning After:

1 Don't wait for him to wake up. Things will be way more awkward if you have to speak to this weirdo. Plus, if he's asleep, you can steal yourself a hoodie, breakfast, cab fare, etc. It's the least he can do for whatever sexy things you did to him last night.

2 If he does wake up, don't try to get him to keep hanging out with you. The night is over. The alcohol has worn off. If he wants to see you again, he can call you when you've taken a shower and brushed your teeth.

3 If he has a roommate who happens to see you on your way out, do not pass go. Do not collect $200. A simple nod of the head is the only politeness you're obligated to express.

Carly Aquilino

> If the guy's awake, you need to say something that you know he would never want to hear. Like, "Oh my God! My kids must be starving! I have to get home now."

THE WALK OF SHAME

So you've made it outside. And yes, you are wearing the little black dress and two-inch heels that you were so proud of last night. And yes, it is a Sunday at eleven am and people are out taking their children to the playground, giving you weird looks like you have something to be ashamed of.

Girl, you have NOTHING to be ashamed of. You got your groove on last night. Walk with your head held high and turn that Walk of Shame into a Stride of Pride. Now that you're out of his house, nobody knows what kind of gargoyle you let touch you. For all they know, you could have hooked up with Ryan Gosling. Or maybe you're dressed so nicely because you're on your way to an awards luncheon where you're being honored with "Most Classy Ass Broad." What do these judgmental bitches on the sidewalks know anyway? It's not like they're virgins. At one point in their lives, before they had kids, these jerks were out doing dirty things, too.

The worst walk of shame to do—but the best one to watch—is the post-Halloween walk of shame. I once had to walk all the way across campus on the morning of November 1st dressed as a slutty lobster. And that walk was a lonely one, during which I thought to myself many times, *Why didn't I dress up as a sleeping bag? Why did I need to craft homemade claws and antennae? What kind of lobster wears fishnets and stilettos anyway?* But then outside my dorm, I ran into my roommate dressed as a slutty Care Bear. Catching one another in the same predicament, we both burst out laughing. She gave me her best Care Bear Stare and I asked her if she'd gotten some tail. (Get it? Tail? Because I was a lobster. Lobster tail! Yeah, it wasn't that funny then either.)

Jamie Lee

Walk of shame is proof that you got some last night. So you own that shit. Girl Code.

WALK OF SHAME

TRIED AND TRUE WAYS TO MAKE HIM LEAVE

Play the Wicked soundtrack	Say, "Let's do it again, but this time I'll be the boy"
Cry	Call your cat your best friend
Invite him to brunch with your parents	Scream, "Who are you and what did you do with my boyfriend?"
Ask if this looks like a yeast infection	Pretend you're your own evil twin
Eat something from the garbage	Fart
Do a Cockney accent	Fake death

So, dear reader, if your Epic Night has turned into a Morning After, don't fret. Walk with purpose, determination, and for God's sakes, don't take your shoes off. You may be having a rough morning, but do not be the barefoot girl. I'll let a lot of things slide, but walking home barefoot is not one of them.

GirlCode:

DON'T TALK, JUST WALK.

GirlCode

Authors

Laura Murphy is the director of Girl Code and writer of many things, including TV shows, commercials, wedding speeches, and embarrassing poetry from junior high. She spent years failing at dating and sex so that you don't have to. You're welcome. Follow her on Twitter @bestlauraever

Sachi Ezura is a comedian, writer, and producer, working in development for MTV2. After graduating from Harvard, she chose to disappoint her parents by pursuing a career in comedy. She produces live shows throughout NYC and co-hosts Comedy at Alligator Lounge, a free stand-up show in Williamsburg every Tuesday. She loves 80s dance parties, attention, her fiancée Jake and her cats Corn & Magoo. She has cried in most public spaces in NYC... is that weird? Follow her on Twitter @misstrionics or read her blog misstrionics.tumblr.com

Brooke Van Poppelen is a NYC based comedian, actress and writer who has appeared on The Late Late Show with Craig Ferguson, Comedy Central, VH1, IFC, MTV and truTV. She's also a writer and producer for Girl Code. brookevanpoppelen.com

Wenonah Hoye is a Brooklyn based writer and editor. She was the editor of *Guy Code: Unleash Your Manhood* and has ghostwritten several books, including a *New York Times* bestselling celebrity memoir.

Chelsea White is a writer, producer, and comedian from Clarion, PA. She's a Producer of MTV's Girl Code and has previously worked off and on camera for VH1, Bravo, TLC and MTV(other), is a contributor for US Weekly and co-host of the popular NYC comedy show 'What Else?' She's also a board member of the Tourette Syndrome Association's NYC Chapter she speaks nationally about her experiences living with the disorder and advocating for others. She lives in NYC with her cat Tanooki. Follow her on Twitter @chelsayuh or visit chelswhite.com